Looking at Teaching Through the Lens of the FFT Clusters

Study Guide
Set 6

Contents

Study Guide Overview

Introduction

Welcome to the FFT (Framework for Teaching) series of Clusters Study Guides. Their purpose is to guide professioncommunities as they engage in activities and discussions to enhance their own practices and the practices of their colleagues. An Instructional Set of lesson artifacts (that may include lesson plans, a video of the entire lesson, student work, and teacher commentary) is used as a resource for each Study Guide. The combination of the Study Guide activities, the Instructional Set artifacts, and the user's experience yields a powerful method of examining teaching and applying learning to one's own practice.

Background

The Instructional Sets are actual lessons led by teachers with their own students. The videos run the duration of the lesson. The teachers and students are not actors, and the lessons are part of their curriculum, not something that was scripted for the Study Guides. The Danielson Group is extremely appreciative of the teachers and their students for providing an opportunity for others to view authentic classroom artifacts for the purpose of professional growth.

A team of educational practitioners and Danielson Group consultants, who have extensive experience in effective teaching practices and professional development training, created this Study Guide series (see Appendix A for the team members). The team received rigorous training on the FFT

Clusters and on how to analyze the teaching and learning evident in the Instructional Sets. They worked with Charlotte Danielson, lead consultants, and each other to create the contents of the Guides.

The series includes many Study Guides. Each Guide was written for a group of accompanying Instructional Sets. The collection includes a sampling of K–12 lessons in Mathematics, English Language Arts, Science, Social Studies, and Science Technology. The majority of lessons are in Mathematics and English Language Arts. Analyzing lessons from a variety of grades and subject areas provides opportunities for educators to stretch their analytic skills and enhance their understanding of the FFT Clusters. A list of the Instructional Sets can be found in Appendix B.

The team created a Record of Evidence for each Instructional Set. The activities portion of the Study Guide provides highlights of the Instructional Set, whereas the Record provides an extensive list of evidence gleaned from the video and artifacts for the FFT Clusters. A Record also includes interpretations of the evidence by the authors who were trained as coders. For each Record, two coders analyzed an Instructional Set independently, then compared their records to produce a composite version for the Study Guide. The Record of Evidence does not contain scores or evaluations, since the evidence is intended for use in professional conversations.

Contents of the Study Guides

Each Study Guide provides a multi-step process for examining the contents of an Instructional Set, reflecting on and discussing its contents, and applying learning from such study to new situations. Each Guide provides the following steps:

Step 1: Lesson Overview

This section provides a high-level summary of the lesson, culled from the video, lesson plans, and artifacts, to provide readers with some background information about the Instructional Set. Many include pre-observation notes in addition to the lesson plans. All lessons are based on rigorous student standards such as the Common Core State Standards (CCSS)/ College and Career Readiness Anchor (CCRA) Standards.

Step 2: Preparation and Questions

Users examine artifacts that the teacher provided as evidence of preparing the lesson. The planning artifacts in an Instructional Set will include the lesson plans and related artifacts such as student assignments, if appropriate. Examining the planning artifacts and jotting down what to look for will help prepare users for viewing the video of the classroom lesson. Users will also generate questions that they have about the artifacts and use those questions when discussing the lesson with their colleagues.

Step 3: Viewing the Classroom Video

Users view the video of the full lesson and note significant behaviors of the teacher and students. Some of the Instructional Sets include samples of student work. The samples were selected by the teacher and do not include teacher comments. If student work is included, users will review it after viewing the video.

Step 4: Selected Highlights of the Lesson Video

This step provides a summary of important teacher and student behaviors that happened in the lesson, and which aspects of the teaching and learning are being exemplified. These noteworthy behaviors will provide users with a lens for their examination of the lesson with their colleagues, and an opportunity to match the highlights with the FFT Clusters.

Step 5: Viewing the Teacher Commentary

Users watch the video of the teacher commentary about the lesson and the students, and jot down noteworthy information. A summary of the commentary and its relationship to effective aspects of teaching are provided.

Step 6: Questions, Applications, and Discussion

Prompts are provided that guide users in analyzing and reflecting on the Instructional Set. This step also includes a set of prompts for thinking about applications to a user's own practice.

Using the Study Guides

The power of professional learning comes when educators can have focused discussions about the teaching and learning that they witness. Individuals can use the Study Guides, but the process of discussing with colleagues what one has learned from the Instructional Set, and how it can be applied to one's own practice, is the action needed to enhance teaching and learning. Just watching videos of effective teachers is not enough to change practice. Additional thinking and actions are needed to effect change. Therefore, the Study Guides are intended for use by educators participating in professional learning communities.

The Guides can be used in any order, but it is recommended that users begin with a grade level and subject area with which they are comfortable.

There are two versions in each Study Guide: one for communities of teachers and one for communities of instructional coaches or mentors of teachers. The first five steps of the process are identical in both versions, and are designed to focus on examining the instruction. A group setting is not necessary for Steps 1–5. They can be completed at an individual's own pace.

Steps 1–5 could be completed as a whole group, though this is not recommended, since interaction is not part of these steps. Watching a 45-minute video is usually best done as an individual activity so the viewer can control the pacing and the volume or elect to wear headphones.

Step 6 requires participants to share their responses, observations, suggestions, and other insights. It is highly recommended that participants work in small groups, so all get an opportunity to contribute to the discussions. The facilitator could select highlights of the small group discussions to share with the whole group.

Step 6 is a group activity, focusing on analyses of the Instructional Set and applications of learning. The activities in Step

6 are similar in the two versions, but the discussions will be different in subtle ways because of the user's role.

Teachers	Instructional Coaches
Communities with all teachers will analyze and reflect on the Instructional Set in Step 6 and will identify an aspect of the learning that went well and another aspect that could be improved. Their colleagues in the community will discuss the analyses and suggest teaching techniques to support student learning as related to the featured lesson. After that activity, the teacher community will think about what they learned from the teacher and lesson, and how they might apply that learning to their own teaching.	*Communities with all coaches/mentors will analyze the Instructional Set in Step 6 and discuss how to prepare for a conversation with the featured teacher. Their colleagues in the community will discuss the analyses and planned questions, comments, and suggestions. Step 6 includes an activity that has the coaches thinking about what they learned from the teacher and lesson, and how they might apply it to their own coaching situation.*

There may be communities comprising educators with different roles, such as a combination of teachers, teacher leaders, and a mentor of beginning teachers. The prompts in Step 6 can be easily modified to accommodate their different roles. There also might be situations where the professional development is done in a whole group setting. Just as with the mixed group learning communities, the prompts and implementation can be modified to support the professional development of all participants.

The Study Guides should be treated as one possible way of using the Instructional Sets for professional growth among educational colleagues. The Guides do not advocate any particular model of coaching or professional learning. If practitioners have a certain model that is used in their district, then they should consider modifying Step 6 to meet their needs or requirements. Additional prompts or steps can be included to support their learning and accommodate their schedules.

Post-Study Activities

Learning communities are encouraged to use the Study Guides as a springboard for creating their own additional professional development activities.

The following example shows an additional set of prompts that could be completed after the learning community completes the activities in Step 6 of the Guide. It serves as a reflective activity and should be done by individuals, then shared with their colleagues.

Here's What, So What, Now What

    a. Here's What: Identify five takeaways from your conversations with your colleagues. What examples did you collect?

    b. *So What:*   How do your takeaways connect to your current practice?

    c. *Now What:*   Based on the takeaways, identify 1–3 next steps you will take to inform your future practice.

Connection to the FFT Clusters

The Study Guides provide information and instructions on how to examine teaching and learning through the lens of the Framework for Teaching (FFT) Clusters. There are three versions of the FFT Clusters document: Generic, Literacy (ELA), and Mathematics. The Generic version reflects those instructional practices that are common across disciplines and was used for these Study Guides. The Literacy and Mathematics versions translate the general language of the narratives and critical attributes, where appropriate, into content-specific language.

Steps 1, 4, and 5 (lesson overview, lesson highlights, and teacher commentary) contain specific information about the Instructional Set and include prompts to match evidence to the related FFT Clusters. It is strongly suggested that copies of the FFT Clusters be available for participants so they can use them during their work with the Study Guides.

Even though the Guides were created with the FFT Clusters in mind, they also can be used to examine the Instructional Sets through the lens of the components of the Framework for Teaching. Practitioners who are familiar with the Framework for Teaching components will find the crosswalk between the Clusters and the components useful. It is located at the beginning of the FFT Clusters document. The FFT Clusters document can be downloaded for free individual use from the Danielson Group website: www.danielsongroup.org.

If practitioners use a different set of teaching standards than the Framework, they will still find the Study Guides and Instructional Sets useful for their professional growth needs. A crosswalk between their teaching standards and the FFT Clusters should be done so practitioners can associate the evidence in the Instructional Sets with their own standards.

Before you begin your examination of an Instructional Set's materials, you may want to check your equipment to make sure you can access the video and artifacts included with the Instructional Set. Enjoy studying the teaching and learning in the Instructional Set, and be prepared to enhance your own practice.

**Looking at Teaching Through
the Lens of the FFT Clusters**

A Study Guide for
Teacher
Learning Communities

Teacher: Braband
Subject: Math
Grade: 10
Topic: The Golden Ratio

Welcome to the Study Guide for the Braband Math Instructional Set, a collection of artifacts and videos for an instructional lesson. This Study Guide provides information and instructions on how to examine teaching and learning through the lens of the Framework for Teaching (FFT) Clusters. In order to complete the steps in this Guide, you will need access to the teacher's planning documents, the lesson video, and the teacher commentary video (http://www.danielsongroup.org/study-guides/). Steps 1–5 of this Study Guide focus on examining the Instructional Set and can be done by an individual. Step 6 is a group activity and focuses on sharing results of the analysis and applications of learning.

Step 1 - Lesson Overview

Read the background information of the lesson provided below.

The teacher of this tenth grade geometry lesson uses mathematical concepts to focus on the golden ratio, a phenomenon widely viewed in nature, art, ancient and modern architecture, and modern day advertising and design. The golden ratio is defined as a special number found by dividing a line into two parts so that the longer part divided by the smaller part is equal to the whole length divided by the longer part. It is often symbolized by using ϕ (phi), after the 21st letter of the Greek alphabet. In an equation form, it looks like this:

$$a/b = (a+b)/a = 1.6180339887498948420$$

Students work in teams in this lesson to discover examples of this, by measuring familiar rectangular-shaped objects in which the length to width ratio equals the golden ratio.

The lesson begins with the familiar routine of reviewing learning and checking homework. The homework assignment on proportions set the stage for the work that the students will be doing in this lesson's activities. The teacher guides the students through carefully selected activities and assignments that are designed to meet the needs of all of her students. She provides worksheets for her right-brained students who need the order and sequence of a worksheet. A video is included in the lesson for those students who are auditory learners, and the opportunity to move around and interact with objects is incorporated for her kinesthetic learners. The lesson culminates with students using their new understanding to not only identify objects in their environment that meet the criteria of the golden ratio, but also to determine the missing dimensions of rectangles that meet the golden ratio criteria.

Ms. Braband reveals in the teacher commentary that this lesson fits into a recently started unit, and that it aligns with the Common Core State Standards (CCSS) Geometry standard on similarity. Previous lessons have focused on helping students understand what a ratio is and how it differs from a proportion. Students have had multiple opportunities apply their understanding by completing homework assignments, working with peers, and working at the board. This lesson provides a different opportunity for students to use their skills and demonstrate their understanding. They will use tools to accurately measure objects, write ratios based on their measurements, and look for a pattern that emerges from these experiences.

Step 2 - Preparation and Questions

- *Read the teacher's lesson plan and jot down things you expect to see and what you want to look for in the video of the lesson.*

- *Write down any questions or comments you have about the lesson plan.*

Step 3 – Viewing the Classroom Video

- *View the complete video, noting those things you expected to see based on the lesson plan. Also note what was missing based on your expectations from the lesson plan. Jot down significant behaviors by the teacher and students pertinent to the FFT Clusters.*

Step 4 – Selected Highlights of the Lesson Video

Read the highlights of the lesson provided below. Note those matching your highlights of the lesson. For each set of statements, determine the FFT Cluster that is best related to the behaviors presented.

The teacher Ms. Braband, guides students in this lesson on a mathematical journey that helps them see the relevancy of mathematics to everyday life. The teacher demonstrates an unwavering commitment and a genuine enthusiasm for the subject she teaches, even when time constraints require modifications to her original plan. She plans and implements a bell-to-bell lesson with a coherent structure that ultimately leads her students to the expected outcome.

A. *The teacher creates a warm and friendly environment with students, while maintaining high expectations for their performance. Although she starts the day joking with the students about Tina Turner, and by warmly greeting a student who enters the room late, she reminds the late student that "timeliness is key." The teacher tells one student who has not completed his homework assignment not to "panic," but she also tells the class that she needs to see "more work" in their homework assignments so that she will know their thought processes. (Cluster ____)*

B. *Clear routines and procedures are established in the classroom that result in little loss of instructional time. The teacher circulates the classroom to check student homework while students are going over the homework assignment on the board. Materials for the lesson are available for quick retrieval and distribution. The teacher distributes supplies for the day to selected students and then tells them to "grab and pass." (Cluster ____)*

C. *The teacher incorporates formative assessment strategies by asking students to hold up their hands if they agree with their classmates' responses. When some students choose to shake their heads instead, the teacher insists that she needs to see hands. The teacher also circulates the room checking students' work as they are working in small groups. (Cluster ____)*

D. *The teacher acknowledges and encourages students to use appropriate academic language when talking about their mathematical understanding. In response to a question, one student says because he was "reducing" it. The teacher thanks the student for using the correct vocabulary. The teacher states, "Four-thirds is a reduction." (Cluster ____)*

E. *The teacher paces the lesson as students progress through the activities in the agenda. She gives the students one minute for certain parts of the agenda but allows additional time when most of the students have not completed a task in the allotted time. (Cluster ____)*

F. *The teacher shows enthusiasm for the content. The teacher tells students that they are going to see how they are going to move from mathematics to beauty. T: For me, it's a no-brainer...but for you it might not be. The teacher concludes the lesson by telling students that now their minds had been "fed a little" and "inspired." She tells students that they are going to go crazy in the next few days trying to figure out what was going on as they made connections from the content to their own lives. The teacher tells the students that the ratio is actually 1.618 and that there are so many things around the world that relate to the golden ratio; e.g. in their backpacks, in their pockets, etc. (Cluster ____)*

G. *The activities and assignments in the lesson have a logical sequence. The teacher tells students that as a conclusion, they are going to look at the worksheets that are at the end of their packets to see if they can relate them to the beginning of the lesson, "try to manipulate pictures to show the golden ratio." (Cluster ____)*

H. *The students are asked to apply their learning at the end of the lesson. Students are asked to work in their differentiated groups to set up a proportion in order to find the missing dimension of a shape or pattern involving the golden ratio. Students need to apply their prior knowledge about ratios and proportions and their new learning about the golden ratio in order to be successful in this task. (Cluster ____)*

Step 5 – Viewing the Teacher Commentary

Watch the video of the teacher's commentary about the lesson and jot down any questions or comments you have about the commentary. Read the highlights below and identify the related FFT Cluster.

A. The teacher talks about the sequence of instruction for this lesson. She explains that the students are about two days into the unit on similarity. She further explains that her students bring a strong background in algebra that has helped prepare them for this extension lesson. The sequence of instruction moves across units from basic algebra; to similarity and proportion of shapes including right triangles; and in this lesson, to looking at rectangles and the golden ratio. This sequence of instruction will prepare students to move on to trigonometry. (Cluster ___)

B. Besides focusing on the concept of the golden ratio, the teacher also focuses this lesson on Core Action 3 that emphasizes the importance of creating an environment of trust and risk-taking. The teacher explains that this has been a focus in her class since the beginning of the school year. The teacher has worked on building a sense of community by paying close attention to seating arrangement and intentionality in grouping of students. She explains that in each group of three students there is a high performing learner, an average learner, and an average to below-average learner. She also states that she makes sure that each group has at least one student who is not afraid to speak out and at least one student who is more quiet and reserved. She has made sure that any student with an IEP is working with at least one student who can provide assistance if needed. She also tries to accommodate the visual, auditory, and kinesthetic learners in her lesson design. She wants all students to have an opportunity to learn without being embarrassed. (Cluster ___)

C. The teacher explains at the end of the commentary that she was pleased at how the students worked together in the lesson, and that the more reserved students could be seen participating in the lesson by measuring objects in their groups. (Cluster ___)

Step 6 – Questions, Applications, and Discussion

The purpose of this step is to prompt your analysis and reflection of the Instructional Set and to have you think about applications to your own practice.

1. Teaching and Learning Related to the FFT Clusters

The purpose of the activity is to increase your understanding of the relationship between the highlights of the Instructional Set and the FFT Clusters. Your identification of an FFT Cluster for each of the highlights is compared to the Cluster identified by the master coders. The Answer Key is located at the end of the activities. You have options on how to complete the comparison. Determine what might work best for your group's learning. Options include, but are not limited to the following.

- Look at the first set of highlights. Take a poll of what each group member identified as the related FFT Cluster. If all members said the same FFT Cluster, have one or two members say why. Compare the group's response to the answer sheet. Repeat for the remainder of the highlights.

OR

- Have each member take one or two highlights. State the correct answer for each one, and a reason why the highlight demonstrates that FFT Cluster. The member will facilitate a discussion if others had different responses, with the goal of having all understand the justification of the correct answer.

OR

- Have members check their own responses to all the highlights. If there are any incorrect answers, then the member selects one highlight and leads a discussion with the group to learn why others think the highlight matches the correct FFT Cluster.

OR

- Determine your own process to check and discuss the match between highlights and the FFT Clusters.

2. **Analysis and Reflection of the Instructional Set**

The purpose of this activity is for you to analyze and reflect on what you saw and heard in the artifacts and videos, to share your analysis with your peers, and to discuss some of the questions or comments you noted. Review the notes, comments, and questions you recorded when you examined the Instructional Set.

- Identify a key teaching and learning attribute demonstrated in the Instructional Set that was effective and state why you think it worked well.

- Identify a different attribute and provide ideas about how it could be enhanced or improved.

- Share your statements with your group and have your peers react to and build upon your analysis and ideas.

Sample statements:

The teacher mentions in the commentary that she has been working on building a strong sense of community within her classroom. Building a sense of community and mutual responsibility is key to fostering effective group work. To that end, the teacher said that she groups students based not only on their academic abilities, but also on personality. She has grouped some of her more reserved students with some of her more confident and verbal students. I noticed that in these group-ings, the teacher has also chosen to have her students work in trios. While I understand that the teacher was able to include a wider range of abilities with three students in the group, she also ran the risk of her quieter students becoming the "odd person out" in a trio. I would encourage this teacher to think about using group roles or other methods to ensure that all students participate and that all voices are heard within the group.

Additional ideas for statements:

- Degree to which students take pride in their work and demonstrate a commitment to mastering challenging content

- Extent to which the instructional strategies used by the teacher are appropriate for the discipline

- Extent to which students monitor their own learning and provide feedback to others

- Extent to which the teacher provides wait time following questions, allowing students time to think and to con-struct an answer

3. **Notice, Learn, and Apply**

The purpose of this activity is for you to reflect on what you learned from your analysis of the Instructional Set and to deter-mine how you will apply it to your teaching.

- Complete the statements:

  "I noticed _____."
  (Insert one thing you noticed about the teacher or students.)

  "And I learned _____."
  (State what you learned related to what you noticed.)

  "I will apply what I learned by _____."
  (Provide example of how you will use what you learned in your own context.)

- Share your statements with your group. Have others react and add how they might apply what you noticed to their own teaching context.

Sample statement:

- I noticed that the teacher kept the lesson moving throughout the entire class period. There was no downtime for any students at the beginning, during, or at the end of the class.

- I learned that it is important for the teacher to pace the lesson so that students are constantly moving towards meeting the instructional outcome established for the lesson.

- I will apply what I learned by sharing the learning outcome and agenda at the beginning of the lesson, and by trying to maintain time limits on each section of the agenda unless there is student evidence that requires some flexibility on my part.

Study Guide for Teachers Answer Key

Highlights from the Lesson Video (Step 4)

A. The teacher creates a warm and friendly environment with students, while maintaining high expectations for their performance. Although she starts the day joking with the students about Tina Turner, and by warmly greeting a student who enters the room late, she reminds the late student that "timeliness is key." The teacher tells one student who has not completed his homework assignment not to "panic," but she also tells the class that she needs to see "more work" in their homework assignments so that she will know their thought processes. (Cluster 2 Safe, Respectful, Supportive, and Challenging Learning Environment)

B. Clear routines and procedures are established in the classroom that result in little loss of instructional time. The teacher circulates the classroom to check student homework while students are going over the homework assignment on the board. Materials for the lesson are available for quick retrieval and distribution. The teacher distributes supplies for the day to selected students and then tells them to "grab and pass." (Cluster 3 Classroom Management)

C. The teacher incorporates formative assessment strategies by asking students to hold up their hands if they agree with their classmates' responses. When some students choose to shake their heads instead, the teacher insists that she needs to see hands. The teacher also circulates the room checking students' work as they are working in small groups. (Cluster 5 Successful Learning by All Students)

D. The teacher acknowledges and encourages students to use appropriate academic language when talking about their mathematical understanding. In response to a question, one student says because he was "reducing" it. The teacher thanks the student for using the correct vocabulary. The teacher states, "Four-thirds is a reduction." (Cluster 2 Safe, Respectful, Supportive, and Challenging Learning Environment)

E. The teacher paces the lesson as students progress through the activities in the agenda. She gives the students one minute for certain parts of the agenda but allows additional time when most of the students have not completed a task in the allotted time. (Cluster 4 Student Intellectual Engagement)

F. The teacher shows enthusiasm for the content. The teacher tells students that they are going to see how they are going to move from mathematics to beauty. T: For me, it's a no-brainer…but for you it might not be. The teacher concludes the lesson by telling students that now their minds had been "fed a little" and "inspired." She tells students that they are going to go crazy in the next few days trying to figure out what was going on as they made connections from the content to their own lives. The teacher tells the students that the ratio is actually 1.618 and that there are so many things around the world that relate to the golden ratio; e.g. in their backpacks, in their pockets, etc. (Cluster 4 Student Intellectual Engagement)

Study Guide for Teachers Answer Key

Highlights from the Lesson Video (Step 4—cont'd.)

G. The activities and assignments in the lesson have a logical sequence. The teacher tells students that as a conclusion, they are going to look at the worksheets that are at the end of their packets to see if they can relate them to the beginning of the lesson, "try to manipulate pictures to show the golden ratio." (Cluster 4 Student Intellectual Engagement)

H. The students are asked to apply their learning at the end of the lesson. Students are asked to work in their differentiated groups to set up a proportion in order to find the missing dimension of a shape or pattern involving the golden ratio. Students need to apply their prior knowledge about ratios and proportions and their new learning about the golden ratio in order to be successful in this task. (Cluster 4 Student Intellectual Engagement)

Study Guide for Teachers Answer Key

Highlights from the Teacher Commentary (Step 5)

A. The teacher talks about the sequence of instruction for this lesson. She explains that the students are about two days into the unit on similarity. She further explains that her students bring a strong background in algebra that has helped prepare them for this extension lesson. The sequence of instruction moves across units from basic algebra; to similarity and proportion of shapes including right triangles; and in this lesson, to looking at rectangles and the golden ratio. This sequence of instruction will prepare students to move on to trigonometry. (Cluster 1 Clarity of Instructional Purpose and Accuracy of Content)

B. Besides focusing on the concept of the golden ratio, the teacher also focuses this lesson on Core Action 3 that emphasizes the importance of creating an environment of trust and risk-taking. The teacher explains that this has been a focus in her class since the beginning of the school year. The teacher has worked on building a sense of community by paying close attention to seating arrangement and intentionality in grouping of students. She explains that in each group of three students there is a high performing learner, an average learner, and an average to below-average learner. She also states that she makes sure that each group has at least one student who is not afraid to speak out and at least one student who is more quiet and reserved. She has made sure that any student with an IEP is working with at least one student who can provide assistance if needed. She also tries to accommodate the visual, au-

ditory, and kinesthetic learners in her lesson design. She wants all students to have an opportunity to learn without being embarrassed. (Cluster 1 Clarity of Instructional Purpose and Accuracy of Content)

C. The teacher explains at the end of the commentary that she was pleased at how the students worked together in the lesson, and that the more reserved students could be seen participating in the lesson by measuring objects in their groups. (Cluster 5 Successful Learning by All Students)

**Looking at Teaching Through
the Lens of the FFT Clusters**

A Study Guide for
Instructional Coach
Learning Communities

Teacher: Braband
Subject: Math
Grade: 10
Topic: The Golden Ratio

Welcome to the Study Guide for the Braband Math Instructional Set, a collection of artifacts and videos for an instructional lesson. This Study Guide provides information and instructions on how to examine teaching and learning through the lens of the Framework for Teaching (FFT) Clusters. In order to complete the steps in this Guide, you will need access to the teacher's planning documents, the lesson video, and the teacher commentary video (http://www.danielsongroup.org/study-guides/). Steps 1–5 of this Study Guide focus on examining the Instructional Set and can be done by an individual. Step 6 is a group activity and focuses on sharing results of the analysis and applications of learning.

Step 1 - Lesson Overview

Read the background information of the lesson provided below.

The teacher of this tenth grade geometry lesson uses mathematical concepts to focus on the golden ratio, a phenomenon widely viewed in nature, art, ancient and modern architecture, and modern day advertising and design. The golden ratio is defined as a special number found by dividing a line into two parts so that the longer part divided by the smaller part is equal to the whole length divided by the longer part. It is often symbolized by using phi, after the 21st letter of the Greek alphabet. In an equation form, it looks like this: a/b = (a+b)/a = 1.6180339887498948420

Students work in teams in this lesson to discover examples of this, by measuring familiar rectangular-shaped objects in which the length to width ratio equals the golden ratio.

The lesson begins with the familiar routine of reviewing learning and checking homework. The homework assignment on proportions set the stage for the work that the students will be doing in this lesson's activities. The teacher guides the students through carefully selected activities and assignments that are designed to meet the needs of all of her students. She provides worksheets for her right-brained students who need the order and sequence of a worksheet. A video is included in the lesson for those students who are auditory learners, and the opportunity to move around and interact with objects is incorporated for her kinesthetic learners. The lesson culminates with students using their new understanding to not only identify objects in their environment that meet the criteria of the golden ratio, but also to determine the missing dimensions of rectangles that meet the golden ratio criteria.

Ms. Braband reveals in the teacher commentary that this lesson fits into a recently started unit, and that it aligns with the Common Core State Standards (CCSS) Geometry standard on similarity. Previous lessons have focused on helping students understand what a ratio is and how it differs from a proportion. Students have had multiple opportunities apply their understanding by completing homework assignments, working with peers, and working at the board. This lesson provides a different opportunity for students to use their skills and demonstrate their understanding. They will use tools to accurately measure objects, write ratios based on their measurements, and look for a pattern that emerges from these experiences.

Step 2 - Preparation and Questions

- *Read the teacher's lesson plan and jot down things you expect to see and what you want to look for in the video of the lesson.*

- *Write down any questions or comments you have about the lesson plan.*

Step 3 – Viewing the Classroom Video

- *View the complete video, noting those things you expected to see based on the lesson plan. Also note what was missing based on your expectations from the lesson plan. Jot down significant behaviors by the teacher and students pertinent to the FFT Clusters.*

Step 4 – Selected Highlights of the Lesson Video

Read the highlights of the lesson provided below. Note those matching your highlights of the lesson. For each set of statements, determine the FFT Cluster that is best related to the behaviors presented.

In this lesson, the teacher Ms. Braband, guides students on a mathematical journey that helps them see the relevancy of mathematics to everyday life. The teacher demonstrates an unwavering commitment and a genuine enthusiasm for the subject she teaches, even when time constraints require modifications to her original plan. She plans and implements a bell-to-bell lesson with a coherent structure that ultimately leads her students to the expected outcome.

A. *The teacher creates a warm and friendly environment with students, while maintaining high expectations for their performance. Although she starts the day joking with the students about Tina Turner, and by warmly greeting a student who enters the room late, she reminds the late student that "timeliness is key." The teacher tells one student who has not completed his homework assignment not to "panic," but she also tells the class that she needs to see "more work" in their homework assignments so that she will know their thought processes. (Cluster ___)*

B. *Clear routines and procedures are established in the classroom that result in little loss of instructional time. The teacher circulates the classroom to check student homework while students are going over the homework assignment on the board. Materials for the lesson are available for quick retrieval and distribution. The teacher distributes supplies for the day to selected students and then tells them to "grab and pass." (Cluster ___)*

C. *The teacher incorporates formative assessment strategies by asking students to hold up their hands if they agree with their classmates' responses. When some students choose to shake their heads instead, the teacher insists that she needs to see hands. The teacher also circulates the room checking students' work as they are working in small groups. (Cluster ___)*

D. *The teacher acknowledges and encourages students to use appropriate academic language when talking about their mathematical understanding. In response to a question, one student says because he was "reducing" it. The teacher thanks the student for using the correct vocabulary. The teacher states, "Four-thirds is a reduction." (Cluster ___)*

E. *The teacher paces the lesson as students progress through the activities in the agenda. She gives the students one minute for certain parts of the agenda but allows additional time when most of the students have not completed a task in the allotted time. (Cluster ___)*

F. *The teacher shows enthusiasm for the content. The teacher tells students that they are going to see how they are going to move from mathematics to beauty. T: For me, it's a no-brainer…but for you it might not be. The teacher concludes the lesson by telling students that now their minds had been "fed a little" and "inspired." She tells students that they are going to go crazy in the next few days trying to figure out what was going on as they made connections from the content to their own lives. The teacher tells the students that the ratio is actually 1.618 and that there are so many things around the world that relate to the golden ratio; e.g. in their backpacks, in their pockets, etc. (Cluster ____)*

G. *The activities and assignments in the lesson have a logical sequence. The teacher tells students that as a conclusion, they are going to look at the worksheets that are at the end of their packets to see if they can relate them to the beginning of the lesson, "try to manipulate pictures to show the golden ratio." (Cluster ____)*

H. *The students are asked to apply their learning at the end of the lesson. Students are asked to work in their differentiated groups to set up a proportion in order to find the missing dimension of a shape or pattern involving the golden ratio. Students need to apply their prior knowledge about ratios and proportions and their new learning about the golden ratio in order to be successful in this task. (Cluster ____)*

Step 5 – Viewing the Teacher Commentary

Watch the video of the teacher's commentary about the lesson and jot down any questions or comments you have about the commentary. Read the highlights below and identify the related FFT Cluster.

A. The teacher talks about the sequence of instruction for this lesson. She explains that the students are about two days into the unit on similarity. She further explains that her students bring a strong background in algebra that has helped prepare them for this extension lesson. The sequence of instruction moves across units from basic algebra; to similarity and proportion of shapes including right triangles; and in this lesson, to looking at rectangles and the golden ratio. This sequence of instruction will prepare students to move on to trigonometry. (Cluster ___)

B. Besides focusing on the concept of the golden ratio, the teacher also focuses this lesson on Core Action 3 that emphasizes the importance of creating an environment of trust and risk-taking. The teacher explains that this has been a focus in her class since the beginning of the school year. The teacher has worked on building a sense of community by paying close attention to seating arrangement and intentionality in grouping of students. She explains that in each group of three students there is a high performing learner, an average learner, and an average to below-average learner. She also states that she makes sure that each group has at least one student who is not afraid to speak out and at least one student who is more quiet and reserved. She has made sure that any student with an IEP is working with at least one student who can provide assistance if needed. She also tries to accommodate the visual, auditory, and kinesthetic learners in her lesson design. She wants all students to have an opportunity to learn without being embarrassed. (Cluster ___)

C. The teacher explains at the end of the commentary that she was pleased at how the students worked together in the lesson, and that the more reserved students could be seen participating in the lesson by measuring objects in their groups. (Cluster ___)

Step 6 – Questions, Applications, and Discussion

The purpose of this step is to prompt your analysis and reflection of the Instructional Set and to have you think about applications to your own practice.

1. **Teaching and Learning Related to the FFT Clusters**

The purpose of the activity is to increase your understanding of the relationship between the highlights of the Instructional Set and the FFT Clusters. Your identification of an FFT Cluster for each of the highlights is compared to the Cluster identified by the master coders. The Answer Key is located at the end of the activities. You have options on how to complete the comparison. Determine what might work best for your group's learning. Options include, but are not limited to the following.

- Look at the first set of highlights. Take a poll of what each group member identified as the related FFT Cluster. If all members said the same FFT Cluster, then have one or two members say why. Compare the group's response to the answer sheet. Repeat for the remainder of the sets of highlights.

OR

- Have each member take one or two sets of highlights and be the discussant for them. The discussant will state the correct answer and state a reason why the statements in the set demonstrate the FFT Cluster. The discussant will facilitate a discussion if members had different responses with the goal of all understanding the justification of the correct answer.

OR

- Have members check their own responses to all the sets of highlights. If there are any incorrect answers, then the member selects one set and leads a discussion with the group to learn why others think the highlights match the correct FFT Cluster.

OR

- Determine your own process to check and discuss the match between highlights and the FFT Clusters.

2. **Analysis and Reflection of the Instructional Set**

The purpose of this activity is for you to analyze and reflect on what you saw and heard in the artifacts and videos and to discuss some of the questions or comments you noted. One element of a professional conversation is asking questions to ascertain more information about a teacher's thinking and the behaviors of both students and teacher. This activity allows you and your peers to practice preparing such questions. Your peers can comment on whether your questions are appropriate and will obtain useful information without making the featured teacher feel uneasy or criticized.

The second part of this activity focuses on helping teachers move their practice forward. Please note that having you prepare for and model an entire conversation about the lesson with the featured teacher is not the purpose of this activity as written. Your group can modify or replace the activity to meet your group's needs

- Review the notes, comments, and questions you recorded when you examined the Instructional Set. Pretend you have the opportunity to ask the teacher some questions to get additional information about the strategies used or decisions made for this Instructional Set.

- Share with your group just the questions you would use with the teacher to elicit additional information. Have your peers comment about your questions and add other questions they had about the same event.

- Share with others in your group what you would do to prompt the teacher's thinking and actions to enhance his/her practice. Take turns sharing and discussing the prompts.

Sample A, Part I:

I noticed that during the lesson, you had to tell at least two groups that they should use the protractor for measuring the pictures in the handouts. These were the groups that had originally measured in inches and you had to tell them that it would be easier if they measured in centimeters. In your commentary, you spoke about students learning to select strategies that would help them be more efficient in their work. What criteria do students use to select one strategy over another?

Sample A, Part II:

Assuming that part of your rationale for grouping students is so they can support each other in their learning, how can you teach students to help each other determine the efficiency of their selected strategies instead of depending on you? Have you tried having students share multiple strategies for solving a problem with the whole class and then discussing which is most efficient? What criteria might students use to determine efficiency?

Sample B, Part I:

You focused on having students make connections to real life by having students predict which items in the room or in their pockets might meet the criteria of the golden ratio. Although you had to modify your original plan by having students measure fewer real-life objects than originally planned, you required students to measure at least two objects. You suggested that one student in the group might assume responsibility for measuring while another student might assume responsibility for performing the calculations. When would it be more "efficient" for you to assign roles for students or to encourage them to do so at the outset of an assignment? What might be some recurring roles that can be defined and routinely included in selected lessons?

Sample B, Part II:

At least two groups seemed to be confused about the difference between a ratio and a proportion during small group work. You had to tell these groups that they did not need to set up a proportion, but instead, determine the ratio of the longest side of the rectangle to the shortest side of the rectangle. In what ways do you keep track of students who may be confused? How do you plan re-teaching for students who may be confused or have misconceptions about previous material? In what ways do you make academic vocabulary a key part of mathematics instruction?

3. Notice, Learn, and Apply

The purpose of this activity is for you to reflect on what you learned from your analysis of the Instructional Set and to determine how you will apply it to your teaching.

- Complete the statements:
  "I noticed _____."
  (Insert one thing you noticed about the teacher or students.)

  "And I learned _____."
  (State what you learned related to what you noticed.)

  "I will apply what I learned by _____."
  (Provide example of how you will use what you learned in your own context.)

- Share your statements with your group. Have others react and add how they might apply what you noticed to their own coaching context.

Sample statements:

- I noticed that the teacher made a conscious effort to make connections to everyday life.

- I learned that making these connections could help students see the relevance of mathematics and engender student enthusiasm for the content.

- I will apply what I learned by having discussions with the teachers that I coach about how Ms. Braband made connections to her students' lives. Then, as I plan with teachers that I coach, I will encourage them to routinely make connections between student learning in mathematics and the everyday experiences of those students.

Study Guide for Instructional Coaches Answer Key
Highlights from the Lesson Video (Step 4)

A. The teacher creates a warm and friendly environment with students, while maintaining high expectations for their performance. Although she starts the day joking with the students about Tina Turner, and by warmly greeting a student who enters the room late, she reminds the late student that "timeliness is key." The teacher tells one student who has not completed his homework assignment not to "panic," but she also tells the class that she needs to see "more work" in their homework assignments so that she will know their thought processes. (Cluster 2 Safe, Respectful, Supportive, and Challenging Learning Environment)

B. Clear routines and procedures are established in the classroom that result in little loss of instructional time. The teacher circulates the classroom to check student homework while students are going over the homework assignment on the board. Materials for the lesson are available for quick retrieval and distribution. The teacher distributes supplies for the day to selected students and then tells them to "grab and pass." (Cluster 3 Classroom Management)

C. The teacher incorporates formative assessment strategies by asking students to hold up their hands if they agree with their classmates' responses. When some students choose to shake their heads instead, the teacher insists that she needs to see hands. The teacher also circulates the room checking students' work as they are working in small groups. (Cluster 5 Successful Learning by All Students)

D. The teacher acknowledges and encourages students to use appropriate academic language when talking about their mathematical understanding. In response to a question, one student says because he was "reducing" it. The teacher thanks the student for using the correct vocabulary. The teacher states, "Four-thirds is a reduction." (Cluster 2 Safe, Respectful, Supportive, and Challenging Learning Environment)

E. The teacher paces the lesson as students progress through the activities in the agenda. She gives the students one minute for certain parts of the agenda but allows additional time when most of the students have not completed a task in the allotted time. (Cluster 4 Student Intellectual Engagement)

F. The teacher shows enthusiasm for the content. The teacher tells students that they are going to see how they are going to move from mathematics to beauty. T: For me, it's a no-brainer...but for you it might not be. The teacher concludes the lesson by telling students that now their minds had been "fed a little" and "inspired." She tells students that they are going to go crazy in the next few days trying to figure out what was going on as they made connections from the content to their own lives. The teacher tells the students that the ratio is actually 1.618 and that there are so many things around the world that relate to the golden ratio; e.g. in their backpacks, in their pockets, etc. (Cluster 4 Student Intellectual Engagement)

G. The activities and assignments in the lesson have a logical sequence. The teacher tells students that as a conclusion, they are going to look at the worksheets that are at the end of their packets to see if they can relate them to the beginning of the lesson, "try to manipulate pictures to show the golden ratio." (Cluster 4 Student Intellectual Engagement)

H. The students are asked to apply their learning at the end of the lesson. Students are asked to work in their differentiated groups to set up a proportion in order to find the missing dimension of a shape or pattern involving the golden ratio. Students need to apply their prior knowledge about ratios and proportions and their new learning about the golden ratio in order to be successful in this task. (Cluster 4 Student Intellectual Engagement)

Study Guide for Instructional Coaches Answer Key
Highlights from the Teacher Commentary (Step 5)

A. The teacher talks about the sequence of instruction for this lesson. She explains that the students are about two days into the unit on similarity. She further explains that her students bring a strong background in algebra that has helped prepare them for this extension lesson. The sequence of instruction moves across units from basic algebra; to similarity and proportion of shapes including right triangles; and in this lesson, to looking at rectangles and the golden ratio. This sequence of instruction will prepare students to move on to trigonometry. (Cluster 1 Clarity of Instructional Purpose and Accuracy of Content)

B. Besides focusing on the concept of the golden ratio, the teacher also focuses this lesson on Core Action 3 that emphasizes the importance of creating an environment of trust and risk-taking. The teacher explains that this has been a focus in her class since the beginning of the school year. The teacher has worked on building a sense of community by paying close attention to seating arrangement and intentionality in grouping of students. She explains that in each group of three students there is a high performing learner, an average learner, and an average to below-average learner. She also states that she makes sure that each group has at least one student who is not afraid to speak out and at least one student who is more quiet and reserved. She has made sure that any student with an IEP is working with at least one student who can provide assistance if needed. She also tries to accommodate the visual, au-ditory, and kinesthetic learners in her lesson design. She wants all students to have an opportunity to learn without being embarrassed. (Cluster 1 Clarity of Instructional Purpose and Accuracy of Content)

C. The teacher explains at the end of the commentary that she was pleased at how the students worked together in the lesson, and that the more reserved students could be seen participating in the lesson by measuring objects in their groups. (Cluster 5 Successful Learning by All Students)

Record of Evidence

This Record of Evidence (ROE) contains key evidence aligned to the FFT Clusters. Interpretive statements about the evidence are also provided. The ROE was created by two master coders who recorded evidence and interpretation statements independently, reviewed each others' work, and arrived at a final composite version based on their professional conversations. This version was reviewed by a leader of the master coders. The ROE is included in this Study Guide so users can see what master coders identified as key evidence, and their interpretation of that evidence through the lens of the FFT Clusters. It is provided as an example of one type of analysis of an Instructional Set. The ROEs were created for professional development rather than evaluative purposes. Users are cautioned about using them for teacher evaluation.

Rubric:	Generic
Grade:	10
Subject:	Math
Topic:	The Golden Ratio
Teacher description:	Female, caucasian, experience unknown
Class description:	There are approximately 30 students in the class. Some students are on IEPs.
Artifacts:	• Two worksheets • Teacher commentary • Instructional plan
Length of video:	47:26

Cluster 1: Clarity of Instructional Purpose and Accuracy of Content

Guiding Questions

- *To what extent does the teacher demonstrate depth of important content knowledge and conduct the class with a clear and ambitious purpose, reflective of the standards for the discipline and appropriate to the students' levels of knowledge and skill?*

- *To what degree are the elements of a lesson (the sequence of topics, instructional strategies, and materials and resources) well designed and executed, and aligned with the purpose of the lesson?*

- *To what extent are they designed to engage students in high-level learning in the discipline?*

Record of Evidence

Cluster 1:   Clarity of Instructional Purpose and Accuracy of Content

Evidence

Instructional Plan and Teacher Commentary
- Learning Goal/Objective: The student will understand and be able to use ratios and proportions to test whether geometric shape, algebraic pattern, or physical object measured will represent the golden ratio.
- Standard: Use ratio and proportion.
- Common Core State Standards (CCSS), Math. Content. HSG-SRT.B.5 – Use congruence and similarity criteria for polygons to solve problems and to prove relationships in geometric figures.
- Essential Targets
  The student will:
  1. solve proportions that apply the golden ratio
  2. recognize shapes or patterns that may involve the golden ratio
  3. apply the lesson to additional practice in homework (from text).
- The teacher also includes a 4-point rubric identifying a goal of Target 3 or higher in the Unit Assessment involving similarity.
- Other assessments:
  1. Checks for understanding throughout the lesson after each set in Worksheet (I, II, III)
  2. Student samples and discussions of findings in Sets I, II on worksheet.
  3. Following day, homework completion
  4. Formative question applied to mid-unit quiz
- Instructional Materials:
  - SmartBoard lesson slides
  - Worksheet
  - Text: Prentice Hall: Mathematics IL Geometry text (2009 edition)
  - Objects in classroom to measure (i.e., posters, shapes, playing cards, everyday items, phone, ID cards, etc.)
  - Tape measures
  - Calculators
- The teacher says in her commentary, "In planning this lesson, I considered where we had been before. We just came out of the chapter on similarity, spent two days setting up proportions, understanding ratios, and are coming out with a prior skill. They have finished Algebra quite strong and most of them are average to above-average learners. I know I can do an extension on the golden ratio because it does incorporate the same skills."
- The teacher states that she will focus on Correction 2 and 3. Correction 2 involves instructional practices to master the content. She has designed three activities to make sure the students have a clear understanding of the content. Correction 3 involves the classroom culture and building a sense of trust. Students have low

Record of Evidence

Cluster 1: Clarity of Instructional Purpose and Accuracy of Content

Evidence (cont'd.)

self-esteem and for them to turn to a neighbor and talk is hard. The teacher set up activities to allow them to talk about mathematic content with each other quietly.

- The teacher explains, "The focus is on the shift of coherence and rigor. We have had a lot of practice in fluency. Need to be fluent and quick, and have done a lot of practice. Brave enough to...helps with rigor to do in different settings. Different opportunity to practice gives them a different sense of mastery."
- The teacher creates pods of students (three students per pod) to differentiate for levels of learning and personality. There are shy learners. "In every lesson, I have to allow them an opportunity to learn and speak math out loud.... "I have very carefully chosen..." e.g., IEP students with students who can help; combining high, average, and average to below; those brave in speaking with quiet and reserved, etc.
- Students can move around the room.
- Activities are scaffolded (left brainers can follow worksheet, video, kinesthetic.) All bases are covered for all types of learners."

Video

- T (during the homework review): Don't get sloppy.
- The teacher tells students to see if they have set up the problem correctly. T: Yesterday, I said....what am I worried about?
- S: Order.
- T: If you don't organize it consistently, you might get a number but it may not fit the problem if your order is off.
- T: Boys, why did you write this?
- S: Because that one is the big one and the right one is the smaller.
- T: Koffie, what's going on there?
- Koffie: Reducing it.
- T: You used the right vocab for that, thank you for that, sir. 4/3 is ….
- T: I'm OK with using your head. What do we do when we use the calculator?
- S: Math 1.
- The teacher works the problem on the white board. T: Tell me what's happening right here.
- S: They cross multiply so it's….
- S: Being reduced, but you don't want a decimal so just leave it as a fraction.
- The teacher explains terminating decimal.
- T: Is that clear? We talked about that yesterday. Decimals as long as they terminate are acceptable.
- (10:43) T (introducing the targets): We need to get our targets out of the way so you understand where we go today. Targets are specific, but an immediate transfer from yesterday's lesson.

Record of Evidence

Cluster 1: Clarity of Instructional Purpose and Accuracy of Content

Evidence (cont'd.)

- Teacher asks students what yesterday's targets were and students answer proportions, ratios. T: We will continue that today…what do we do with them, why do we need them?
- The teacher leads a review of yesterday's targets. Targets are on the SmartBoard. Teacher reads and students record.

Group 1 Activity
- T: Let's get going. Everyone have a measurement tool. Again, you are going to need a calculator today.
- Students work and teacher interrupts. T: I am OK with grabbing a calculator, typing it in as a division problem. Today it can be a decimal rounded up to the nearest tenth. Three minutes or less.
- S to S: What are we setting it equal to? I don't get that.
- T: Just the ratio, not the proportion.
- The teacher tells the students they are noticing all kinds of centering around a certain number. Teacher explains relation and that the ratio will become the golden ratio.
- T: Write this down. What's going on here? You are going to start seeing it out there all of the time. The ratio is actually 1.618. Look in your pockets, backpacks. There are so many things out there, it's kind of crazy, that's why I'm teaching math.

Group 2 Activity
- Teacher introduces the second activity with a Ted Talk about the golden ratio.
- The teacher gives directions modified from the lesson plan. T: On the worksheet, it says five, we are going to do two, we don't have the time. Turn to the worksheet. I've provided enough info so that if some of you want to rock and roll, go; or you might all go together. Get at least two or more. See if you can find in this room somewhere if you can find a golden rectangle. If not, I want to see your mistake in the room.
- Students get right to work. Teacher continues to give ideas of what to measure.
- S: I am just going to guess at this. We can just say 7.
- Two pairs measure the board. Other students stay at their desk. The teacher continues to coax them to move around the classroom.
- T: What we need to do now is we need to make sure that your eye will be somewhat trained a little bit. You understand that it is almost 1 to 1 a little more than 1.5…taking this side, putting it up here….explains.
- The teacher gives students directions for the last activity. T: Turn in your worksheet to the back page. Now that your minds have been fed and inspired and you understand that it's visible, you are going to go crazy out there. This is a conspiracy

Record of Evidence

Cluster 1: Clarity of Instructional Purpose and Accuracy of Content

Evidence (cont'd.)

and someone planned. It started at the beginning of time. Is it just our eye? Nature? Most aesthetically pleasing ratio. Look at the worksheets and turn it into the golden ratio. Look at example 1…quiet time to read example 1, please.

• Student work on the problem, no clarifying questions are asked.

Interpretation

• The lesson plan is clear, aligns with the Common Core State Standards (CCSS), and is appropriate for the students' level of knowledge.

• The teacher demonstrates a depth of content knowledge, and knowledge of the sequence of learning within the unit.

• The activities and presentation of content are designed, delivered, and executed to engage students in high-level learning. All materials and resources are sufficient to engage the students in the activities.

• The strategies are appropriate to the students' and activities.

Record of Evidence

Cluster 2: Safe, Respectful, Supportive, and Challenging Learning Environment

Guiding Questions

- *To what extent do the interactions between teacher and students, and among students, demonstrate genuine caring and a safe, respectful, supportive, and also challenging learning environment?*

- *Do teachers convey high expectations for student learning and encourage hard work and perseverance? Is the environment safe for risk taking?*

- *Do students take pride in their work and demonstrate a commitment to mastering challenging content?*

Evidence

- The teacher is working at the SmartBoard with one student before class begins. T: Lets carry it to these guys, maybe they can give suggestions. Good start.

- The teacher greets the students and they respond. She shares a story about a gift and then asks if they are tired, to which they respond with a "yeah."

- The teacher talks to a student individually. T: Do you have what you need from me? Did your mom get that email? Perfect.

- The teacher refers to Blocks Logic and asks students, "Is she a favorite of yours? The answer would be yes 'cause she's a favorite of mine." Students reply with a "yes."

- T (to a late student): Felicia, good morning. Timeliness is key.

- As the teacher is checking individual students' homework, one student forgot two problems and teacher says, "That's OK, don't panic about that."

- The teacher says good morning to three students as she checks homework.

- The teacher exchanges personal comments with students. T: It is warm. John, how can you squeeze it all in there? S to T: We match. T: We match, coordination level there, buddy. Nice job on the effort of the homework.

- Two students respond to other students: "You are so off, it is frustrating me so much." "Whoa. I told you to hold it up so I could measure it."

- The teacher encourages the students to move around during the last activity. T: Get up and move, move, move. Ss: Geez. T: People are you slow today?

- The teacher encourages the students to persevere. T: What did you measure? Whoa, we are finding golden everywhere. T: You asked if you could do it in your head. Think about your assessment and all I can see is an answer, I can't give you points. I need to see your work. We aren't just testing the fundamental, we are going further on that. I need to see that communication going on.

Record of Evidence

Cluster 2: **Safe, Respectful, Supportive, and Challenging Learning Environment**

Evidence (cont'd.)

- The teacher explains to the students they might be just a "smidgen" off, but that's OK.
- T: I had one student ask does this have anything to do with Fibonacci. Boom, you are there.

Interpretation

- The interaction between teacher and students and among students is generally respectful and safe.

- The teacher reminds students of expectations and standards of conduct.

- The learning environment is challenging and the teacher conveys high expectations for student learning. The teacher thanks the students for working and trying. The teacher insists that students persevere and everyone tries even if the answers are not correct. The students show pride in their work by volunteering to go to the board and by answering questions.

Record of Evidence

Cluster 3: Classroom Management
Guiding Questions

- *Is the classroom well run and organized?*

- *Are classroom routines and procedures clear and carried out efficiently by both teacher and students with little loss of instructional time?*

- *To what extent do students themselves take an active role in their smooth operation?*

- *Are directions for activities clearly explained so that there is no confusion?*

- *Do students not only understand and comply with standards of conduct, but also play an active part in setting the tone for maintaining those standards?*

- *How does the physical environment support the learning activities?*

Evidence
- There are at least 30 students in the classroom, sitting at desks facing the front of the room. Student desks are arranged in pods with three students in each pod.
- The teacher reminds students of the routine behaviors. T: Do we have any takers on this? You can bring a partner. Any takers? I am not going to do from scratch. You know how I go. Just grab and pass. Please write down, you know how the routine goes.
- The teacher reminds students of standards of conduct as she gives directions. T: Don't get distracted and play with it, please. And just hold on to these and don't fiddle with the tools. Let's put our stuff to the side. Be patient.
- The teacher waits for students to quick talking. T: Silence is not golden right now.
- The teacher uses procedures to asses prior knowledge and agreement, and to gain their attention. T: Head shakes, yes or no? In the center, yes or no? Head shakes in the left, yes or no? (Students vote to agree or disagree.)
- T: I need you back (holds up fist and students are quiet). Eyes on me, on me, and thank you.
- The teacher tells the students to leave their protractors and things on their desks at the end of the lesson.

Record of Evidence

Cluster 3:   Classroom Management

Interpretation

- The classroom is well run and organized. The routines are established and the students know what is expected. The teacher insists the students adhere to the routines and take responsibility for the efficient classroom.

- There is little loss of instructional time as students move from whole group work to pod work.

- The agenda for the lesson and directions for activities are clear, and there is no confusion.

- Student behavior is entirely appropriate; any student misbehavior is very minor and swiftly handled.

- The physical environment is conducive to small group activity and to large group work.

Record of Evidence

Cluster 4: Student Intellectual Engagement

Guiding Questions

- *To what extent are students intellectually engaged in a classroom of high intellectual energy?*

- *What is the nature of what students are doing?*

- *Are they being challenged to think and make connections through both the instructional activities and the questions explored?*

- *Do the teacher's explanations of content correctly model academic language and invite intellectual work by students?*

- *Are students asked to explain their thinking, to construct logical arguments citing evidence, and to question the thinking of others?*

- *Are the instructional strategies used by the teacher suitable to the discipline, and to what extent do they promote student agency in the learning of challenging content?*

Evidence

- One student is working on a problem at the board before the lesson begins. T: Lets carry it to these guys, maybe they can give suggestions. Good start.
- The lesson begins with a whole-group review at the SmartBoard. The teacher asks students to come to the board and work the problem while she checks homework. T: Tell me what's happening right here.
- S: They cross multiply so it's….
- The teacher explains and works on the SmartBoard.
- T: Hands up, what's going on here? Mattie?
- S: Being reduced, but you don't want a decimal so just leave it as a fraction.
- The teacher explains terminating decimal. T: Is that clear? We talked about that yesterday. Decimals as long as they terminate are acceptable.
- S: What's the word?
- T: That's OK
- S: Is a repeating decimal acceptable?
- T: Yes. We're going to push that rule today. Not to confuse you. We're going to use that a little differently today.
- T: Any questions on these two? Wait—good job.
- Teacher connects the quote to what they are doing. T: See how we are talking about beauty when we are talking about mathematics? For me it's a no-brainer, but for you it might not be.
- The teacher calls for volunteers to use these values. T: I need volunteers to use these values. Here are the values, there are the proportions, rewritten in not that order. Who is up? I need one to write in a different order.
- Mattie and John go to the SmartBoard and work the problems. Students disagree with John's calculations; teacher asks students to rework; students vote and agree.

Record of Evidence

Cluster 4: Student Intellectual Engagement

Evidence (cont'd.)

Group Activity 1
- The teacher connects their work with exceptional art, music, etc. found on the worksheet. T (giving directions): Let's get going. Does everyone have a measurement tool? Start with the worksheet, read with me or just listen. (The teacher reads the directions.)
- Students work and teacher interrupts. T: I am OK with grabbing a calculator, typing it in as a division problem. Today it can be a decimal rounded up to the nearest tenth. Three minutes or less.
- S to S: What are we setting it equal to? I don't get that. T: Just the ratio, not the proportion.
- Some students are working together and others are working on their own. All students are engaged. Teacher moves from group to group, answering questions.
- The teacher gives the students one more minute and then clarifies which is more accurate, inches or centimeters.
- Teacher demonstrates how to measure and gives the students more time. T: Let's see how many we can measure. Speed up your time, long by short. Grab your calculator and tell me what you get. S: 1.5.
- The teacher asks for the students' attention to make an adjustment.
- Teacher asks for answers. T: You may be a smidgen off, that's a mathematical term, but that's OK. Our goal is to... (students are talking in the background). What is the conversion point?
- Teacher splits the room up in three groups, with each group working separate problems.
- Teacher extends the time so students reach understanding.

Group Activity 2
- The teacher tells the students to make sure their eyes will be somewhat trained to understand that it is "almost 1 to 1, a little more than 1.5, taking this side, putting it up here."
- The teacher changes the assignment to complete two problems rather than five because there is not enough time.
- T: See if you can find in this room somewhere if you can find a golden rectangle. If not, I want to see your mistake.
- Most students get right to work. The teacher continues to give ideas of things to measure. Some students do not move and the teacher perseveres in getting them moving and measuring.
- T: If you found the wrong one, that's OK, write it down. I just want your eye to look around. We are finding golden everywhere. Finish up, we have more learnin' to do.
- (42:59) The teacher tells student to find their seats.

Record of Evidence

Cluster 4: Student Intellectual Engagement

Evidence (cont'd.)

- T (to the whole group): What did you try? Students share what they measured.
- The teacher tells the students to turn to the back page of the worksheet. The teacher continues to model the explanation of content, academic language, and intellectual work.
- T: Now that your minds have been fed and inspired and you understand that it's visible. You are going to go crazy out there. This is a conspiracy and someone planned. It started at the beginning of time. Is it just our eye? Nature? Most aesthetically pleasing ratio. Look at the worksheets and turn it into the golden ratio. Look at example 1…quiet time to read example 1, please.
- Students worked individually.
- The teacher draws a rectangle on the board and asks Kirk what to do. The student explains.
- Felicia: Why do we put it over 1? A student explains.
- The teacher finishes the problem and the bell rings.
- T: Enjoy your day, leave your protractors and things on your desk. Enjoy your weekend, well done.

Interpretation

- All students are engaged at some level during the lesson. The activities (homework review, activities 1 and 2, and the concluding task) were designed so all students are engaged.

- The teacher uses art, architecture, things in the room, items in students' pockets, etc. to make a connection to the students.

- The teacher models academic language. The activities and questioning invite intellectual work by the students.

- Students explain their thinking and the teacher accepts answers that are wrong.

- The strategies were suitable to the discipline, and the teacher modified the lesson according to the students' understanding.

Record of Evidence

Cluster 5:   Successful Learning by All Students
Guiding Questions

- *To what extent does the teacher ensure learning by all students?*

- *Does the teacher monitor student understanding through specifically designed questions or instructional techniques?*

- *To what extent do students monitor their own learning and provide respectful feedback to classmates?*

- *Does the teacher make modifications in presentations or learning activities where necessary, taking into account the degree of student learning?*

- *Has the teacher sought out other resources (including parents) to support students' learning?*

- *In reflection, is the teacher aware of the success of the lesson in reaching students?*

Evidence
- The teacher includes Rubric/Assessment in the Instructional Plan (Target 3 or higher met on Unit Assessment involving similarity). Other assessments included:
  1. Check for understanding throughout the lesson after each set in Worksheet (I, II, III)
  2. student samples and discussions of findings in Set I & II on worksheet
  3. following day, homework completion
  4. formative-question applied to mid-unit quiz.
- During homework review, the teacher asks student, "And again, boys, Koffie, can you do just one?"
- T: What's going on here, do you have what you need? When you find the other one, show it to me.
- T: Nice job on the homework. What do we need to push? S: Draw a picture, more work.
- The teacher tells students they can do it in their heads, but to think about assessment. If all she can see is an answer, she can't give points. T: I need to see your work.
- The teachers asks the students to process the problem, and match it with their work to see if it is set up correctly. Students talk. T: Let me focus on their work a little bit. Let's chat.
- T: Boys, why did you write this? Koffie, what's going on there?
- Teacher introduces the targets and checks for understanding. T: What do we do with our proportions? S: Compare them for similar shapes. T: When we need something, what do we do?

Record of Evidence

Cluster 5:   Successful Learning by All Students

Evidence (cont'd.)

- Student answers correctly. Teacher asks students to shake their heads, yes or no if they know.
- Students volunteer to go to the board to do another version of the problem: rewrite it in a different order. Students raise their hands in agreement with Mattie's work. John calculates the problem. The teacher tells students to "check, check, check." Students do not agree with John. Students work the problem and agree.

Group Activity 1
- While the students work in groups, the teacher monitors their understanding, walking from table to table and asking questions.
- The teacher stops the group work to make an adjustment (clarification) to ensure all students understand. T: You may be a smidgen off, that's a mathematical term, but that's OK.
- Teacher extends the time for completion so that all students reach understanding.
- T: What did you guys get? Good. Anybody over here got it? What did you get? 21? That is not a square. What did you measure?
- The teacher draws the students' attention to the front of the room. T: What you are noticing is that we are all kind of centering around a certain number. I had one student ask does this have anything to do with Fibonacci. Boom, you are there.
- Students have the opportunity to measure any item, and some students relate the golden ratio to personal items.
- The teacher connects the golden ratio to several items, ranging in date from the Parthenon to Apple.

Group Activity 2
- The teacher modifies the lesson because they are running out of time. She makes this modification to ensure all students understand the concept.
- The teacher tells students to look at example 1, read, and relate to the beginning activity. The teacher draws the rectangle on the SmartBoard and asks Kirk what to do. Kirk explains the problem.
- Felicia: Why do we put it over 1? The student explains.
- The teacher finishes the problem and the bell rings.
- T: Enjoy your day, leave your protractors and things on your desk. Enjoy your weekend, well done.

Record of Evidence

Cluster 5:   Successful Learning by All Students

Interpretation

- The formative assessments are aligned to the learning outcomes.

- The teacher monitors the students' understanding of homework before moving on to today's lesson. The teacher monitors student learning during the lesson, questioning both individuals and groups of students.

- The teacher modifies the lesson, ensuring that students understand the concepts before moving on.

- The teacher gives the students a strategy to check their work and reminds them to "check, check, check."

Record of Evidence

Cluster 6: Professionalism

Guiding Questions

- *To what extent does the teacher engage with the professional community (within the school and beyond) and demonstrate a commitment to ongoing professional learning?*

- *Does the teacher collaborate productively with colleagues and contribute to the life of the school?*

- *Does the teacher engage in professional learning and take a leadership role in the school to promote the welfare of students?*

Evidence

No evidence of Cluster 6 is present in this Instructional Set.

FFT Clusters Study Guide: Set 6 (Math 10)

**Looking at Teaching Through
the Lens of the FFT Clusters**

A Study Guide for
Teacher
Learning Communities

Teacher: Scurr
Subject: ELA
Grade: 5
Topic: Comparing and Contrasting
Across Texts

Welcome to the Study Guide for the Scurr ELA Instructional Set, a collection of artifacts and videos for an instructional lesson. This Study Guide provides information and instructions on how to examine teaching and learning through the lens of the Framework for Teaching (FFT) Clusters. In order to complete the steps in this Guide, you will need access to the teacher's planning documents, the lesson video, and the teacher commentary video (http://www.danielsongroup.org/study-guides/). Steps 1–5 of this Study Guide focus on examining the Instructional Set and can be done by an individual. Step 6 is a group activity and focuses on sharing results of the analysis and applications of learning.

Step 1 - Lesson Overview

Read the background information of the lesson provided below.

This English Language Arts lesson focuses on comparing and contrasting similar articles and is designed to be connected to recent social studies discussions of explorers and small pox. The lesson plan notes the diversity of the students' academic abilities. Planned turn-and-talk questions as well as open-ended activities are differentiated to address this diversity.

Students independently read two nonfiction articles in this lesson: "The Mystery of the Messy Desk," an article about Albert Fleming; and "The Speckled Monster," an article about the small pox vaccine. Students use a graphic organizer to compare and contrast the ideas presented in each article.

Students had previously read the two articles, and have coded "The Speckled Monster." They are instructed to get out "The

Mystery of the Messy Desk" article and quietly re-read/skim and code for 5–10 minutes to "activate their thinking."

Students are then directed to turn and talk to a neighbor. Whole group sharing and discussion is also planned. Poster paper is distributed for students to map differences and similarities between the articles, to note key unfamiliar or seldom-used vocabulary, and to generate "big ideas" from the two articles.

The teacher has provided a plan that includes lesson modifications, and a set of teacher and student artifacts to assist an observer in understanding her plans and student work. Copies of the two articles, yellow coding cards, and large poster paper are provided to students as materials/resources for the activity. The teacher commentary video provides support for a deeper understanding of the lesson.

This lesson is aligned to Common Core State Standards, with a focus on comparing and contrasting similar articles about scientific breakthroughs. The following two standards, when met, will help demonstrate depth of important content knowledge:

- RI.5.5 Compare and contrast the overall structure of events, ideas, concepts, or information in two or more texts noted for this lesson.

- RI.5.4 Determine the meaning of general academic and domain-specific words and phrases in a text relevant to a grade 5 topic or subject area.

Mrs. Scurr conducts the class with expectations reflective of the standards. Questions posed are suitable for clarification purposes.

This lesson plan addresses individual student needs. For example, one student has some difficulty with handwriting and often uses his laptop to record ideas. Ms Scurr will offer the student this option. She will also have a pre-created organizer for him to use if he prefers to write ideas down. The student can also ask a peer or teacher to scribe for him. The lesson plan addresses differentiated instruction for all students, the grouping of students, an engagement activity, formative assessments, and summative assessment that are to be incorporated into the lesson.

 ### Step 2 - Preparation and Questions

- *Read the teacher's lesson plan and jot down things you expect to see and what you want to look for in the video of the lesson.*

- *Write down any questions or comments you have about the lesson plan.*

 ### Step 3 – Viewing the Classroom Video

- *View the complete video, noting those things you expected to see based on the lesson plan. Also note what was missing based on your expectations from the lesson plan. Jot down significant behaviors by the teacher and students pertinent to the FFT Clusters.*

4

Step 4 – Selected Highlights of the Lesson Video

Read the highlights of the lesson provided below. Note those matching your highlights of the lesson. For each set of statements, determine the FFT Cluster that is best related to the behaviors presented.

A. Students in this lesson will compare and contrast similar informational articles about scientific break-throughs. Students previously will have read and coded the article, "The Speckled Monster," and will re-read "The Mystery of the Messy Desk" at the beginning of this lesson. Students will code while re-reading, to check for understanding and to activate their thinking. They will make their thinking visible while coding their reading. After re-reading, students will do a turn-and-talk activity at their table groups and articulate their thinking. Mrs. Scurr will provide open-ended question prompts on the turn-and-talk cards to generate collaborative dialogue. (Cluster ___)

B. Each student will create a map of similarities and differences between the two articles on the poster paper provided, using the "Adventures Across the Texts" organizer. Students will use words or pictures to share their thinking on the organizer. Students will be called on to share their work with the whole group. (Cluster ___)

C. The teacher models academic language and invites intellectual work by students. She shares a model for the poster activity prior to students completing the assignment on their own. Similarities and differences are shared, as well as what the expectations are for the vocabulary part ("not dictionary definitions"). Students are instructed to summarize "the big idea." Five differences are noted as required, but the teacher shares with students that she did the assignment herself and was able to come up with ten. This challenges her students to also go beyond the minimum requirement. (Cluster ___)

D. The teacher puts example of a graphic organizer on the board. Everyone is to receive poster paper. A chart is divided horizontally with three sections, with two sections divided and labeled for both articles. (Cluster ___).

E. The The teacher involves students in the activity's directions. T: What organizer do we typically use for similarities and differences? (Cluster ___)

F. Teacher circulates around the room, checking for understanding of individual students and of group thinking. (Cluster ___)

G. Students individually write their ideas on their chart. Students are asked to explain their thinking and upon occasion, cite evidence from the text (both texts are out during the activity). Students share answers to the sample on the displayed Venn diagram. They note five differences between the texts, five similarities, and list new vocabulary in words/pictures. They summarize the "big idea." (Cluster ___)

H. The teacher demonstrates a high regard for student abilities, including that of working with a partner. One student is observed covering his ears, perhaps to eliminate multiple conversations impacting his ability to concentrate. Mrs. Scurr uses close proximity and prompts to encourage his active participation. Although others are observed complying with her directions, he is not observed recording anything on paper. (Cluster ___)

I. Routines and procedures are clear and carried out by both teacher and students with little loss of instructional time. Students move quickly and quietly from small group interactions to whole class discussion and are free to work standing or sitting. (Cluster ___)

Step 5 – Viewing the Teacher Commentary

5

Watch the video of the teacher's commentary about the lesson and jot down any questions or comments you have about the commentary. Read the highlights below and identify the related FFT Cluster.

A. Mrs. Scurr states that they have just begun practicing comparing and contrasting across texts, so this is a new skill for the students. She says, "This is the second or third time they have used nonfiction texts." She shares that her students are just getting comfortable with the process. (Clusters ___ and ___)

B. Mrs. Scurr mentions that one shift (or modification) is in the use of the graphic organizer. She has tiered the chart intentionally to address the abilities of all students. Additionally, to "dive deeper today," she shares how her plans were structured to meet individual needs by having students read the texts either with a partner or with her. She acknowledges that she is "getting her feet wet with comparing and contrasting texts." She describes giving students the turn-and-talk cards and cues to promote engagement with their partner during that activity. (Cluster ___)

C. Mrs. Scurr plans her thinking around specific students who might benefit from the turn-and-talk strategy. She wants everyone in the class to participate and uses the activity to support this goal. (Clusters ___ and ___)

D. Mrs. Scurr's lesson modification to includes all students in activities demonstrate a high regard for student abilities. One student has difficulty with partner work completion, regulating his voice level, and verbal sounds. The teacher uses proximity to help keep one student at ease. Prompts are provided to enable his participation within the group conversation. He is given a pre-created organizer with highlighting of the expectations for him. This one student may only complete the contrasting article section. (Cluster ___)

Step 6 – Questions, Applications, and Discussion

The purpose of this step is to prompt your analysis and reflection of the Instructional Set and to have you think about applications to your own practice.

1. **Teaching and Learning Related to the FFT Clusters**

The purpose of the activity is to increase your understanding of the relationship between the highlights of the Instructional Set and the FFT Clusters. Your identification of an FFT Cluster for each of the highlights is compared to the Cluster identified by the master coders. The Answer Key is located at the end of the activities. You have options on how to complete the comparison. Determine what might work best for your group's learning. Options include, but are not limited to the following.

- Look at the first set of highlights. Take a poll of what each group member identified as the related FFT Cluster. If all members said the same FFT Cluster, have one or two members say why. Compare the group's response to the answer sheet. Repeat for the remainder of the highlights.

OR

- Have each member take one or two highlights. State the correct answer for each one, and a reason why the highlight demonstrates that FFT Cluster. The member will facilitate a discussion if others had different responses, with the goal of having all understand the justification of the correct answer.

OR

- Have members check their own responses to all the highlights. If there are any incorrect answers, then the member selects one highlight and leads a discussion with the group to learn why others think the highlight matches the correct FFT Cluster.

OR

- Determine your own process to check and discuss the match between highlights and the FFT Clusters.

2. **Analysis and Reflection of the Instructional Set**

The purpose of this activity is for you to analyze and reflect on what you saw and heard in the artifacts and videos, to share your analysis with your peers, and to discuss some of the questions or comments you noted. Review the notes, comments, and questions you recorded when you examined the Instructional Set.

- Identify a key teaching and learning attribute demonstrated in the Instructional Set that was effective and state why you think it worked well.

- Identify a different attribute and provide ideas about how it could be enhanced or improved.

- Share your statements with your group and have your peers react to and build upon your analysis and ideas.

Sample statements:

I noticed that most of the students participated in the lesson. There was one male student who left the classroom during the lesson and was unable to complete the assignment. This student had difficulty with partner work completion, regulating his voice level, and verbal sounds. The teacher used proximity to help keep one student at ease. Prompts are provided to enable his participation within the group conversation. Proximity seemed to be beneficial, and I would continue its continued use. Providing differentiation for this particular student will support his learning.

Additional ideas for statements:

- Degree to which students take pride in their work and demonstrate a commitment to mastering challenging content

- Extent to which the instructional strategies used by the teacher are appropriate for the discipline

- Extent to which students monitor their own learning and provide feedback to others

- Extent to which the teacher provides wait time following questions, allowing students time to think and to construct an answer

3. **Notice, Learn, and Apply**

The purpose of this activity is for you to reflect on what you learned from your analysis of the Instructional Set and to determine how you will apply it to your teaching.

- Complete the statements:
  "I noticed _____."
  (Insert one thing you noticed about the teacher or students.)

  "And I learned _____."
  (State what you learned related to what you noticed.)

  "I will apply what I learned by _____."
  (Provide example of how you will use what you learned in your own context.)

- Share your statements with your group. Have others react and add how they might apply what you noticed to their own teaching context.

Sample statement:

- I noticed the teacher had the students do a turn-and-talk at their table groups, sharing their thinking about open-ended questions created by the teacher.

- I learned that students need prompts to begin the conversation, to challenge their thinking, and to make connections.

- I will apply what I learned during this literacy lesson across various content areas when I make connections to previous readings and discussions and when I challenge students' thinking.

Study Guide for Teachers Answer Key

Highlights from the Lesson Video (Step 4)

A. Students in this lesson will compare and contrast similar informational articles about scientific breakthroughs. Students previously will have read and coded the article, "The Speckled Monster," and will re-read "The Mystery of the Messy Desk" at the beginning of this lesson. Students will code while re-reading, to check for understanding and to activate their thinking. They will make their thinking visible while coding their reading. After re-reading, students will do a turn-and-talk activity at their table groups and articulate their thinking. Mrs. Scurr will provide open-ended question prompts on the turn-and-talk cards to generate collaborative dialogue. (Cluster 4 Student Intellectual Engagement)

B. Each student will create a map of similarities and differences between the two articles on the poster paper provided, using the "Adventures Across the Texts" organizer. Students will use words or pictures to share their thinking on the organizer. Students will be called on to share their work with the whole group. (Cluster 4 Student Intellectual Engagement)

C. The teacher models academic language and invites intellectual work by students. She shares a model for the poster activity prior to students completing the assignment on their own. Similarities and differences are shared, as well as what the expectations are for the vocabulary part ("not dictionary definitions"). Students are instructed to summarize "the big idea." Five differences are noted as required, but the teacher shares with

students that she did the assignment herself and was able to come up with ten. This challenged her students to also go beyond the minimum requirement. (Cluster 4 Student Intellectual Engagement)

D. The teacher puts example of a graphic organizer on the board. Everyone is to receive poster paper. A chart is divided horizontally with three sections, with two sections divided and labeled for both articles. (Cluster 1 Clarity of Instructional Purpose and Accuracy of Content)

E. The teacher involves students in the activity's directions. T: What organizer do we typically use for similarities and differences? (Cluster 4 Student Intellectual Engagement)

F. Teacher circulates around the room, checking for understanding of individual students and of group thinking. (Cluster 5 Successful Learning by All Students)

G. Students individually write their ideas on their chart. Students are asked to explain their thinking and upon occasion, cite evidence from the text (both texts are out during the activity). Students share answers to the sample on the displayed Venn diagram. They note five differences between the texts, five similarities, and list new vocabulary in words/pictures. They summarize the "big idea. (Cluster 4 Student Intellectual Engagement)

H. The teacher demonstrates a high regard for student abilities, including that of working with a partner. One

FFT Clusters Study Guide: Set 6 (ELA 5)

Study Guide for Teachers Answer Key

Highlights from the Lesson Video (Step 4—cont'd.)

student is observed covering his ears, perhaps to eliminate multiple conversations impacting his ability to concentrate. Mrs. Scurr uses close proximity and prompts to encourage his active participation. Although others are observed complying with her directions, he is not observed recording anything on paper. (Cluster 2 Safe, Respectful, Supportive, and Challenging Learning Environment)

I. Routines and procedures are clear and carried out by both teacher and students with little loss of instructional time. Students move quickly and quietly from small group interactions to whole class discussion and are free to work standing or sitting. (Cluster 3 Classroom Management)

Study Guide for Teachers Answer Key

Highlights from the Teacher Commentary (Step 5)

A. Mrs. Scurr states that they have just begun practicing comparing and contrasting across texts, so this is a new skill for the students. She says, "This is the second or third time they have used nonfiction texts." She shares that her students are just getting comfortable with the process. (Cluster 1 Clarity of Instructional Purpose and Accuracy of Content and Cluster 5 Successful Learning by All Students)

B. Mrs. Scurr mentions that one shift (or modification) is in the use of the graphic organizer. She has tiered the chart intentionally to address the abilities of all students. Additionally, to "dive deeper today," she shares how her plans were structured to meet individual needs by having students read the texts either with a partner or with her. She acknowledges that she is "getting her feet wet with comparing and contrasting texts." She describes giving students the turn-and-talk cards and cues to promote engagement with their partner during that activity. (Cluster 1 Clarity of Instructional Purpose and Accuracy of Content)

C. Mrs. Scurr plans her thinking around specific students who might benefit from the turn-and-talk strategy. She wants everyone in the class to participate and uses the activity to support this goal. (Cluster 1 Clarity of Instructional Purpose and Accuracy of Content and Cluster 4 Student Intellectual Engagement)

D. Mrs. Scurr's lesson modification to includes all students in activities demonstrate a high regard for student abilities. One student has difficulty with partner work completion, regulating his voice level, and verbal sounds. The teacher uses proximity to help keep one student at ease. Prompts are provided to enable his participation within the group conversation. He is given a pre-created organizer with highlighting of the expectations for him. This one student may only complete the contrasting article section. (Cluster 2 Safe, Respectful, Supportive, and Challenging Learning Environment)

**Looking at Teaching Through
the Lens of the FFT Clusters**

A Study Guide for
Instructional Coach
Learning Communities

Teacher: Scurr
Subject: ELA
Grade: 5
Topic: Comparing and Contrasting
Across Texts

Welcome to the Study Guide for the Scurr ELA Instructional Set, a collection of artifacts and videos for an instructional lesson. This Study Guide provides information and instructions on how to examine teaching and learning through the lens of the Framework for Teaching (FFT) Clusters. In order to complete the steps in this Guide, you will need access to the teacher's planning documents, the lesson video, and the teacher commentary video (http://www.danielsongroup.org/study-guides/). Steps 1–5 of this Study Guide focus on examining the Instructional Set and can be done by an individual. Step 6 is a group activity and focuses on sharing results of the analysis and applications of learning.

Step 1 - Lesson Overview

Read the background information of the lesson provided below.

This English Language Arts lesson focuses on comparing and contrasting similar articles and is designed to be connected to recent social studies discussions of explorers and small pox. The lesson plan notes the diversity of the students' academic abilities. Planned turn-and-talk questions as well as open-ended activities are differentiated to address this diversity.

In this lesson, students independently read two nonfiction articles: "The Mystery of the Messy Desk," an article about Albert Fleming; and "The Speckled Monster," an article about the small pox vaccine. Students use a graphic organizer to compare and contrast the ideas presented in each article.

Students had previously read the two articles, and have coded "The Speckled Monster." They are instructed to get out "The

Mystery of the Messy Desk" article and quietly re-read/skim and code for 5–10 minutes to "activate their thinking."

Students are then directed to turn and talk to a neighbor. Whole group sharing and discussion is also planned. Poster paper is distributed for students to map differences and similarities between the articles, to note key unfamiliar or seldom-used vocabulary, and to generate "big ideas" from the two articles.

The teacher has provided a plan that includes lesson modifications, and a set of teacher and student artifacts to assist an observer in understanding her plans and student work. Copies of the two articles, yellow coding cards, and large poster paper are provided to students as materials/resources for the activity. The teacher video provides support for a deeper understanding of the lesson.

This lesson is aligned to Common Core standards, with a focus on comparing and contrasting similar articles about scientific breakthroughs. The following two standards, when met, will help demonstrate depth of important content knowledge:

- RI.5.5 Compare and contrast the overall structure of events, ideas, concepts, or information in two or more texts noted for this lesson.

- RI.5.4 Determine the meaning of general academic and domain-specific words and phrases in a text relevant to a grade 5 topic or subject area.

Mrs. Scurr conducts the class with expectations reflective of the standards. Questions posed were suitable for clarification purposes.

This lesson plan addresses individual student needs. For example, one student has some difficulty with handwriting and often uses his laptop to record ideas. Teacher will offer student this option. Teacher will also have a pre-created organizer for him to use if he prefers to write ideas down. The student can also ask a peer or teacher to scribe for him). The lesson plan addresses differentiated instruction for all students, the grouping of students, an engagement activity, formative assessments, and summative assessment that are to be incorporated into the lesson.

Step 2 - Preparation and Questions

- *Read the teacher's lesson plan and jot down things you expect to see and what you want to look for in the video of the lesson.*

- *Write down any questions or comments you have about the lesson plan.*

Step 3 – Viewing the Classroom Video

- *View the complete video, noting those things you expected to see based on the lesson plan. Also note what was missing based on your expectations from the lesson plan. Jot down significant behaviors by the teacher and students pertinent to the FFT Clusters.*

4

Step 4 – Selected Highlights of the Lesson Video

Read the highlights of the lesson provided below. Note those matching your highlights of the lesson. For each set of statements, determine the FFT Cluster that is best related to the behaviors presented.

A. Students in this lesson will compare and contrast similar informational articles about scientific breakthroughs. Students previously will have read and coded the article, "The Speckled Monster," and will re-read "The Mystery of the Messy Desk" at the beginning of this lesson. Students will code while re-reading, to check for understanding and to activate their thinking. They will make their thinking visible while coding their reading. After re-reading, students will do a turn-and-talk activity at their table groups and articulate their thinking. Mrs. Scurr will provide open-ended question prompts on the turn-and-talk cards to generate collaborative dialogue. (Cluster ___)

B. Each student will create a map of similarities and differences between the two articles on the poster paper provided, using the "Adventures Across the Texts" organizer. Students will use words or pictures to share their thinking on the organizer. Students will be called on to share their work with the whole group. (Cluster ___)

C. The teacher models academic language and invites intellectual work by students. She shares a model for the poster activity prior to students completing the assignment on their own. Similarities and differences are shared, as well as what the expectations are for the vocabulary part ("not dictionary definitions"). Students are instructed to summarize "the big idea." Five differences are noted as required, but the teacher shares with students that she did the assignment herself and was able to come up with ten. This challenges her students to also go beyond the minimum requirement. (Cluster ___)

D. The teacher puts example of a graphic organizer on the board. Everyone is to receive poster paper. A chart is divided horizontally with three sections, with two sections divided and labeled for both articles. (Cluster ___).

E. The The teacher involves students in the activity's directions. T: What organizer do we typically use for similarities and differences? (Cluster ___)

F. Teacher circulates around the room, checking for understanding of individual students and of group thinking. (Cluster ___)

G. Students individually write their ideas on their chart. Students are asked to explain their thinking and upon occasion, cite evidence from the text (both texts are out during the activity). Students share answers to the sample on the displayed Venn diagram. They note five differences between the texts, five similarities, and list new vocabulary in words/pictures. They summarize the "big idea." (Cluster ___)

H. The teacher demonstrates a high regard for student abilities, including that of working with a partner. One student is observed covering his ears, perhaps to eliminate multiple conversations impacting his ability to concentrate. Mrs. Scurr uses close proximity and prompts to encourage his active participation. Although others are observed complying with her directions, he is not observed recording anything on paper. (Cluster ___)

I. Routines and procedures are clear and carried out by both teacher and students with little loss of instructional time. Students move quickly and quietly from small group interactions to whole class discussion and are free to work standing or sitting. (Cluster ___)

5

Step 5 – Viewing the Teacher Commentary

Watch the video of the teacher's commentary about the lesson and jot down any questions or comments you have about the commentary. Read the highlights below and identify the related FFT Cluster.

A. Mrs. Scurr states that they have just begun practicing comparing and contrasting across texts, so this is a new skill for the students. She says, "This is the second or third time they have used nonfiction texts." She shares that her students are just getting comfortable with the process. (Clusters ____ and ____)

B. Mrs. Scurr mentions that one shift (or modification) is in the use of the graphic organizer. She has tiered the chart intentionally to address the abilities of all students. Additionally, to "dive deeper today," she shares how her plans were structured to meet individual needs by having students read the texts either with a partner or with her. She acknowledges that she is "getting her feet wet with comparing and contrasting texts." She describes giving students the turn-and-talk cards and cues to promote engagement with their partner during that activity. (Cluster ____)

C. Mrs. Scurr plans her thinking around specific students who might benefit from the turn-and-talk strategy. She wants everyone in the class to participate and uses the activity to support this goal. (Clusters ____ and ____)

D. Mrs. Scurr's lesson modification to includes all students in activities demonstrate a high regard for student abilities. One student has difficulty with partner work completion, regulating his voice level, and verbal sounds. The teacher uses proximity to help keep one student at ease. Prompts are provided to enable his participation within the group conversation. He is given a pre-created organizer with highlighting of the expectations for him. This one student may only complete the contrasting article section. (Cluster ____)

Step 6 – Questions, Applications, and Discussion

The purpose of this step is to prompt your analysis and reflection of the Instructional Set and to have you think about applications to your own practice.

1.   **Teaching and Learning Related to the FFT Clusters**

The purpose of the activity is to increase your understanding of the relationship between the highlights of the Instructional Set and the FFT Clusters. Your identification of an FFT Cluster for each of the highlights is compared to the Cluster identified by the master coders. The Answer Key is located at the end of the activities. You have options on how to complete the comparison. Determine what might work best for your group's learning. Options include, but are not limited to the following.

- Look at the first set of highlights. Take a poll of what each group member identified as the related FFT Cluster. If all members said the same FFT Cluster, then have one or two members say why. Compare the group's response to the answer sheet. Repeat for the remainder of the sets of highlights.

OR

- Have each member take one or two sets of highlights and be the discussant for them. The discussant will state the correct answer and state a reason why the statements in the set demonstrate the FFT Cluster. The discussant will facilitate a discussion if members had different responses with the goal of all understanding the justification of the correct answer.

OR

- Have members check their own responses to all the sets of highlights. If there are any incorrect answers, then the member selects one set and leads a discussion with the group to learn why others think the highlights match the correct FFT Cluster.

OR

- Determine your own process to check and discuss the match between highlights and the FFT Clusters.

2. **Analysis and Reflection of the Instructional Set**

The purpose of this activity is for you to analyze and reflect on what you saw and heard in the artifacts and videos and to discuss some of the questions or comments you noted. One element of a professional conversation is asking questions to ascertain more information about a teacher's thinking and the behaviors of both students and teacher. This activity allows you and your peers to practice preparing such questions. Your peers can comment on whether your questions are appropriate and will obtain useful information without making the featured teacher feel uneasy or criticized.

The second part of this activity focuses on helping teachers move their practice forward. Please note that having you prepare for and model an entire conversation about the lesson with the featured teacher is not the purpose of this activity as written. Your group can modify or replace the activity to meet your group's needs

- Review the notes, comments, and questions you recorded when you examined the Instructional Set. Pretend you have the opportunity to ask the teacher some questions to get additional information about the strategies used or decisions made for this Instructional Set.

- Share with your group just the questions you would use with the teacher to elicit additional information. Have your peers comment about your questions and add other questions they had about the same event.

- Share with others in your group what you would do to prompt the teacher's thinking and actions to enhance his/her practice. Take turns sharing and discussing the prompts.

Sample A, Part I:

You did a wonderful job of engaging the students in the creation of their "Adventures Across the Text" organizer charts. You asked them to compare and contrast the two articles they read and to explain their thinking, citing specific examples and noting key vocabulary and big ideas.

It appeared that the students looked to you as facilitator to orchestrate the interactions. How conscious were you of this? Do you think they are ready for more of a facilitator role, to ask questions of other students or offer comments directly? What criteria would you look for or need to teach, so that students might be ready for a facilitator role and to ask questions of other students?

Sample A, Part II:

I know it is something of a challenge, but I think there are a few students in your class who, if given the prompt, would ask question of their peers. How might rotating the role of discussion facilitator help push the discussion? Do you think discussion could be sustained by the students, with some teacher interjections at critical spots? What knowledge or skills might students need in order for them to be able to facilitate the discussion? How might you go about teaching that knowledge or those skills? What might you use as criteria to determine when to interject?

Sample B, Part I:

The prompt for this discussion was comparing and contrasting similar informational articles about scientific breakthroughs. I wonder, however, if the turn-and-talk prompt questions and the "Adventures Across the Text" tiered graphic organizer served to deepen students' understanding around the key vocabulary and the big ideas.

For example, there are certain terms that are repeated several times in both articles. Do you think that the students could explore this at a deeper level? How do you determine what are "critical terms" and what are "nice to know" terms? What evidence might let you know that students are ready to explore at a deeper level?

Sample B, Part II:

How might you prompt and support student thinking and discussion about "the big idea," or ideas that both authors want to convey in these two articles? When would have been a good time to transition them to such a deeper exploration? What criteria might be used to discern when transitioning would be appropriate? Will there be lessons in the near future where you can try those techniques? As you consider upcoming lessons, when might you be able to try those techniques?

3. **Notice, Learn, and Apply**

The purpose of this activity is for you to reflect on what you learned from your analysis of the Instructional Set and to determine how you will apply it to your teaching.

- Complete the statements:
  "I noticed _____."
  (Insert one thing you noticed about the teacher or students.)

  "And I learned _____."
  (State what you learned related to what you noticed.)

  "I will apply what I learned by _____."
  (Provide example of how you will use what you learned in your own context.)

- Share your statements with your group. Have others react and add how they might apply what you noticed to their own coaching context.

Sample statements:

- I noticed the teacher had the students do a turn-and-talk at their table groups, sharing their thinking about open-ended questions created by the teacher.

- I learned that students need prompts to begin the conversation, to challenge their thinking, and to make connections. I have not seen many teachers use this strategy, nor require students to explain their thinking.

- I will share this strategy with other teachers that I'm coaching. I think it would also work for teachers of mathematics and science, where teacher-created questions also challenge student thinking and help students make connections.

Study Guide for Instructional Coaches Answer Key
Highlights from the Lesson Video (Step 4)

A. Students in this lesson will compare and contrast similar informational articles about scientific breakthroughs. Students previously will have read and coded the article, "The Speckled Monster," and will re-read "The Mystery of the Messy Desk" at the beginning of this lesson. Students will code while re-reading, to check for understanding and to activate their thinking. They will make their thinking visible while coding their reading. After re-reading, students will do a turn-and-talk activity at their table groups and articulate their thinking. Mrs. Scurr will provide open-ended question prompts on the turn-and-talk cards to generate collaborative dialogue. (Cluster 4 Student Intellectual Engagement)

B. Each student will create a map of similarities and differences between the two articles on the poster paper provided, using the "Adventures Across the Texts" organizer. Students will use words or pictures to share their thinking on the organizer. Students will be called on to share their work with the whole group. (Cluster 4 Student Intellectual Engagement)

C. The teacher models academic language and invites intellectual work by students. She shares a model for the poster activity prior to students completing the assignment on their own. Similarities and differences are shared, as well as what the expectations are for the vocabulary part ("not dictionary definitions"). Students are instructed to summarize "the big idea." Five differences are noted as required, but the teacher shares with

students that she did the assignment herself and was able to come up with ten. This challenged her students to also go beyond the minimum requirement. (Cluster 4 Student Intellectual Engagement)

D. The teacher puts example of a graphic organizer on the board. Everyone is to receive poster paper. A chart is divided horizontally with three sections, with two sections divided and labeled for both articles. (Cluster 1 Clarity of Instructional Purpose and Accuracy of Content)

E. The teacher involves students in the activity's directions. T: What organizer do we typically use for similarities and differences? (Cluster 4 Student Intellectual Engagement)

F. Teacher circulates around the room, checking for understanding of individual students and of group thinking. (Cluster 5 Successful Learning by All Students)

G. Students individually write their ideas on their chart. Students are asked to explain their thinking and upon occasion, cite evidence from the text (both texts are out during the activity). Students share answers to the sample on the displayed Venn diagram. They note five differences between the texts, five similarities, and list new vocabulary in words/pictures. They summarize the "big idea. (Cluster 4 Student Intellectual Engagement)

H. The teacher demonstrates a high regard for student abilities, including that of working with a partner. One student is observed covering his ears, perhaps to eliminate multiple conversations impacting his ability to concentrate. Mrs. Scurr uses close proximity and prompts to encourage his active participation. Although others are observed complying with her directions, he is not observed recording anything on paper. (Cluster 2 Safe, Respectful, Supportive, and Challenging Learning Environment)

I. Routines and procedures are clear and carried out by both teacher and students with little loss of instructional time. Students move quickly and quietly from small group interactions to whole class discussion and are free to work standing or sitting. (Cluster 3 Classroom Management)

Study Guide for Instructional Coaches Answer Key
Highlights from the Teacher Commentary (Step 5)

A. Mrs. Scurr states that they have just begun practicing comparing and contrasting across texts, so this is a new skill for the students. She says, "This is the second or third time they have used nonfiction texts." She shares that her students are just getting comfortable with the process. (Cluster 1 Clarity of Instructional Purpose and Accuracy of Content and Cluster 5 Successful Learning by All Students)

B. Mrs. Scurr mentions that one shift (or modification) is in the use of the graphic organizer. She has tiered the chart intentionally to address the abilities of all students. Additionally, to "dive deeper today," she shares how her plans were structured to meet individual needs by having students read the texts either with a partner or with her. She acknowledges that she is "getting her feet wet with comparing and contrasting texts." She describes giving students the turn-and-talk cards and cues to promote engagement with their partner during that activity. (Cluster 1 Clarity of Instructional Purpose and Accuracy of Content)

C. Mrs. Scurr plans her thinking around specific students who might benefit from the turn-and-talk strategy. She wants everyone in the class to participate and uses the activity to support this goal. (Cluster 1 Clarity of Instructional Purpose and Accuracy of Content and Cluster 4 Student Intellectual Engagement)

D. Mrs. Scurr's lesson modification to includes all students in activities demonstrate a high regard for student abilities. One student has difficulty with partner work completion, regulating his voice level, and verbal sounds. The teacher uses proximity to help keep one student at ease. Prompts are provided to enable his participation within the group conversation. He is given a pre-created organizer with highlighting of the expectations for him. This one student may only complete the contrasting article section. (Cluster 2 Safe, Respectful, Supportive, and Challenging Learning Environment)

Record of Evidence

This Record of Evidence (ROE) contains key evidence aligned to the FFT Clusters. Interpretive statements about the evidence are also provided. The ROE was created by two master coders who recorded evidence and interpretation statements independently, reviewed each others' work, and arrived at a final composite version based on their professional conversations. This version was reviewed by a leader of the master coders. The ROE is included in this Study Guide so users can see what master coders identified as key evidence, and their interpretation of that evidence through the lens of the FFT Clusters. It is provided as an example of one type of analysis of an Instructional Set. The ROEs were created for professional development rather than evaluative purposes. Users are cautioned about using them for teacher evaluation.

Rubric:	Generic
Grade:	5
Subject:	ELA
Topic:	Comparing and Contrasting Across Texts
Teacher description:	Female, caucasian
Class description:	23 regular education students total: 12 male, 11 female; 2 IEP's and one 504 plan; No ELL Students; 5 Project Arrow (academically talented students); 6 students participate in reading intervention program to boost comprehension and fluency.
Artifacts:	• Lesson plan • Yellow Coding Card for each student • "Adventures Across Texts" Graphic Organizer Tiered Chart (2 for classroom examples) • Turn-and-talk cards • "The Mystery of the Messy Desk" article • "The Speckled Monster" article • Across the Text student work charts • Teacher video commentary
Length of video:	53:31

Record of Evidence

Cluster 1: Clarity of Instructional Purpose and Accuracy of Content

Guiding Questions

- *To what extent does the teacher demonstrate depth of important content knowledge and conduct the class with a clear and ambitious purpose, reflective of the standards for the discipline and appropriate to the students' levels of knowledge and skill?*

- *To what degree are the elements of a lesson (the sequence of topics, instructional strategies, and materials and resources) well designed and executed, and aligned with the purpose of the lesson?*

- *To what extent are they designed to engage students in high-level learning in the discipline?*

Evidence

Instructional Plan
- Teacher provides a detailed lesson plan listing classroom demographics, lesson focus, topic and text, lesson and materials set up, lesson modifications, lesson reflection, and "What you should know about my lesson and classroom."
- Lesson is aligned to Common Core State Standards, with the focus on comparing and contrasting similar articles about scientific breakthroughs.
- Lesson modification: One student has difficulty with partner work completion, regulating his voice level, and verbal sounds. Teacher will use proximity to help keep student at ease. Prompts are provided to him so he is able to participate in group conversations. A pre-created organizer will be given to him, noting in high-lighted marker what the expectations are for him. This student may only complete the contrasting article section.
- Students have previously read the two articles and have coded "The Speckled Monster." They are instructed to get out "The Mystery of the Messy Desk" article and to quietly re-read/skim and code it for 5-10 minutes to "activate their thinking."
- Students are then directed to turn and talk to a neighbor. Whole group sharing and discussion is also planned.
- Poster paper is distributed for students to map differences and similarities between the articles, note key vocabulary (words they don't know or haven't used in conversations), and to note some "big ideas" generated from the two articles.
- Teacher shares her reflective thoughts regarding how the standards are being met. In "what you should know about my lesson and classroom," she mentions playing soothing music while her students are working independently, and providing study carrels for students to minimize distractions. She notes that one student may "throw me a curve ball" during this lesson and she has prepared to differentiate for his needs if this is the case.

Record of Evidence

Cluster 1:   Clarity of Instructional Purpose and Accuracy of Content

Evidence (cont'd.)

Teacher Commentary
- The teacher explains that they have just begun to compare and contrast across texts, so this is a new skill for the students, one with which they are just getting comfortable. This is the second or third time they have used non-fiction texts.
- Teacher states that one of the shifts she made is to the graphic organizer. She tiered the chart intentionally to meet the needs of all students.
- Teacher acknowledges that she is getting her feet wet with comparing and contrasting texts.
- Teacher shared how her plans were structured to meet individual student needs by having some students read the texts with a partner or with her, in order "to dive deeper today." She notes giving them the turn-and-talk cards to facilitate engagement with their partner.
- Teacher wants everyone in the class to participate in the activity. She used the turn-and-talk activity to support this goal.

Classroom Video
- T: Pull out the "Mystery of the Messy Desk" that you read yesterday on your own. We did not do any coding yesterday. I am going to give 5–8 minutes to do a quicker re-read. Code or annotate this time.
- T: Share your thinking in the column. Will help you remember what you were thinking at that time.
- T: Right Thomas?
- (1:07) Teacher provides images on SMART Board. T: Will be interesting to see if you can figure out which picture goes with what article.
- T: 5–8 quiet minutes, writing utensil, "Messy Desk" article, and coding card. Get started.
- Students are seated in desks groups of five.
- T: (to male student previously not engaged): I don't see any marks on your paper and you read this yesterday. S: (inaudible response, but appears to be an excuse).
- T: I know you were thinking when you read this but I don't see anything. We'll do that later. I need you to do this now.
- Teacher jokes with another male student about a non-fiction book. Later, she rolls her eyes with a female student after a discussion about blue cheese having a type of safe mold that some eat. Teacher returns to the group where the one male student (navy shirt) was not actively engaged in the assignment and asks if he read about something he already knew. He shrugs his shoulders and cover his ears, which appear to be red.
- 8:25: Teacher pulls the class back together and introduces the turn-and-talk exercise. She asks questions like "What was surprising? Perplexing?" T (to a male student): What were the most important ideas? Student then asks his partner.

Record of Evidence

Cluster 1: Clarity of Instructional Purpose and Accuracy of Content

Evidence (cont'd.)

- Female student is heard, "Alexander found mold/bacteria."
- T: I'm hearing good conversation—reading between the lines.
- T: Why does the author use words like inoculate, vaccine, without varying their word choices?
- Emma: Since young people are to read it?
- Annalisa: Words are very important?
- Ethan: They are science words?
- Teacher further explores why a disease is noted as a speckled monster. Several responses address her question, including Shotsy (male): "The disease was gobbling up the population."
- Teacher relates a recent social studies lesson about the European explorers bringing small pox to the Indians in the New World.
- (13:50) Female student stands at the desk of the boy in the navy turtle neck shirt who was not actively engaged in the assignment. After she speaks with him and leaves, he follows her and departs the classroom at 14:23.
- (21:18) Teacher explains what is needed for the poster activity: two articles, pens/markers, and a large sheet of poster paper that each will receive for the next part of the lesson.
- T: Set it up like this (showing an example) with three horizontal sections. Differences (list 5) – Similarities (list 5) – New vocabulary experienced (you can define, but not using a dictionary or draw it), and the last section is for the big idea—looking at the articles as a whole…what are the lessons/big picture the author is conveying?
- (29:21) One person/table group picks up the poster papers for their table group and all begin work. As students begin to use rulers and prepare their large paper, the teacher says they don't have to have lines for writing their responses.
- T: I'm more concerned about your thoughts. As students begin to work, the teacher begins to single out on-task students. T: Thomas is making good use of his time. Haley is getting good thoughts down on paper.
- (33:28) Teacher moves around to the individual tables again, checking their work and addressing any questions students may have. One male student notes he is having trouble expressing what he wants to say. The teacher asks him to explain his thoughts to her and she helps him summarize them for the poster paper. T: You had it in you all along!
- T: (to a female student): Very good. You are very observant!
- Teacher says to another female student that on her chart she is making parallel comparisons with the two texts, noting that she doesn't think anyone else has done so (a positive comment).

Record of Evidence

Cluster 1: Clarity of Instructional Purpose and Accuracy of Content

Evidence (cont'd.)

- (44:50) All charts are filled in to some degree, except for the student who left the room. Teacher continues to check in with her students as she moves around to various tables.
- T (to male student): Can you be more specific? What in science?
- (48:45) T: We may need to finish tomorrow. Can you listen to me while you are working?
- Students respond yes.
- Teacher asks the difference between bacteria and virus. Several responses indicate an understanding of the differences/similarities.
- T: Thumbs up if you got to the similarity portion of your chart.
- The second (similarity) section was to completed after teacher review/approval of their first (differences) section.
- T: Put this inside sheet like a folder and take the table stack…one person per group…to the round table.
- Class period ends.

Record of Evidence

Cluster 1:   Clarity of Instructional Purpose and Accuracy of Content

Interpretation

- Teacher video, comprehensive lesson plan, teacher artifacts, and student work are helpful for the observer.

- The purpose for today's lesson was shared in the teacher video interview, lesson plan, and at the beginning of the classroom video.

- Meeting the two standards noted for this lesson helps demonstrate depth of important content knowledge. Additionally, the teacher conducts the class with expectations reflective of the standards. Questions posed were suitable for clarification purposes.

- Lesson elements were sequenced appropriately to build skills in understanding of coding, questioning, comparing and contrasting two texts, noting new vocabulary, and identifying the big idea for both chosen texts.

- The teacher notes having planned for her academically diverse classroom, e.g., choosing specific turn-and-talk questions to further the understanding of certain students in the class.

- Though she tried several times to get a student to put something on paper and to orally share his thoughts about the reading, he was basically non-committal, shrugging his shoulders or doing something the teacher said would occur later. I might ask the teacher if this was typical behavior for him? Or how does she know he has learned the goals/objectives for this lesson? I might also explore ideas about how to address this student with other observers of this video.

Record of Evidence

Cluster 2: Safe, Respectful, Supportive, and Challenging Learning Environment

Guiding Questions

- *To what extent do the interactions between teacher and students, and among students, demonstrate genuine caring and a safe, respectful, supportive, and also challenging learning environment?*

- *Do teachers convey high expectations for student learning and encourage hard work and perseverance? Is the environment safe for risk taking?*

- *Do students take pride in their work and demonstrate a commitment to mastering challenging content?*

Evidence

- (1:25) Teacher calls student by name. T: Right, Thomas.

- (3:24) Teacher circulates the room. T: I see a lot of great remarks and coding marks that people are marking down.

- Teacher conveys expectations for all students by asking them to compare and contrast the overall structure of events, ideas, concepts, and information in two texts. Two similar informational articles about scientific breakthroughs, "The Mystery of the Messy Desk" and "The Speckled Monster" are the selected non-fiction articles.

- (00:13) T: Everybody pull out "The Mastery of the Messy Desk" article.

- (00:33) Teacher gives students time to do a re-read. T: On your own, I want you to do a quicker re-read or skim, and code and annotate. Share your thinking in the column. So about 5–8 minutes.

- (6:02) T: If you finished, you can go back and code again to see if there are things you missed.

- Little instructional time is lost in transitioning from whole group work to individual work.

- (1:18) Students, seated in table groups of 4–5, immediately began working on their reading assignment, using a writing instrument, "Messy Desk" article, and coding card.

- Teacher asks for volunteer to respond to her questions. Students participate willingly and appear confident in offering their ideas in front of classmates.

- (3:21) T: If you have any questions, I will come to you. Teacher circulates the room, helping students.

- Soothing music is playing in the background as students work on their charts.

Record of Evidence

Cluster 2: Safe, Respectful, Supportive, and Challenging Learning Environment

Evidence (cont'd.)

- All ideas expressed are accepted without criticism. Students complete the various aspects of the lesson, culminating with the individual poster projects (some samples are shared by the teacher).

- A male student uses a ruler to make lines for writing text on his poster vs. doing it freehand. A female student who runs out of room wants to add on another piece of poster paper. The teacher suggests that she just add the last part on the side. Student didn't appear pleased, but proceeded with the teacher's suggestion.

- Students work to master the content of the lesson, with the exception of one male student who did not record any information during the first half of the class period when he was present. The teacher continues to prompt him to record his thoughts from the previous day's reading.

- T: What was surprising? What was perplexing?

- T: Why is this important learning about his messy desk?

- T: Why is the disease referred as a speckled monster?

- T (to male student): You had it in you all the time!

- T (to female student): Very good; you are very observant!

- T (to class): Can you listen to me while you are working? Class responds respectfully, in unison, "Yes."

- Teacher states in post conference video that she designed the lesson to be rigorous and challenging for all her students. They all used the same two texts, regardless of their ability.

Record of Evidence

Cluster 2: Safe, Respectful, Supportive, and Challenging Learning Environment

Interpretation

- Lesson Plan Reflection section outlines all 3 Core Action Indicators that will be visible in the lesson.

- The teacher makes productive changes to the lesson plan in response to evidence of student difficulties as she tiers the tasks to meet the challenges of all students.

- The environment appears to be safe for risk taking since all ideas expressed are accepted without criticism.

- Students seem to take pride in their work (using a ruler to make lines for writing vs. doing it freehand; student who wants to add on another piece of poster paper).

Record of Evidence

Cluster 3:   Classroom Management
Guiding Questions

- *Is the classroom well run and organized?*

- *Are classroom routines and procedures clear and carried out efficiently by both teacher and students with little loss of instructional time?*

- *To what extent do students themselves take an active role in their smooth operation?*

- *Are directions for activities clearly explained so that there is no confusion?*

- *Do students not only understand and comply with standards of conduct, but also play an active part in setting the tone for maintaining those standards?*

- *How does the physical environment support the learning activities?*

Evidence
- The classroom has student work displayed (hanging snowmen mobiles), posters, a calendar, and a SmartBoard. Classroom has 5 groups of tables with 5 desks to a group. Students and teacher can easily move around the classroom.
- The physical environment is a support system for the learning activities. Materials are readily available for the students to use. The teacher notes in her lesson plan that she will have extra copies of the articles and notes during the lesson. If students need pens or markers, they are to let her know and she will provide them.
- (3:55) Teacher circulates the room and checks in with one student. T: I don't see any marks on your page. Right now, I need to see your thinking. I know that you were thinking while you were reading. Student begins to work.
- Directions appear to be clear; students do not appear confused about what they are to do.
- (6:15) T: Can I see thumbs up if you're on second page or past?
- Students shows their thumbs immediately.
- T: Three minutes"
- (7:45) T: Ladies and gentlemen, on your desk you have a yellow turn-and-talk card. There are five questions you could use. You don't have to use all of them; You can ask your neighbor two or three questions about what you read. What was surprising, new or interesting; something you were able to visualize? I want you to do turn-and-talk. You might have a pair or group of three. I will set the timer and then come back together as a group.
- (9:03) Teacher sets the timer for 5 minutes.
- T: I will let you choose.
- (9:18) Transition from whole group to small group work. Transition is smooth as students begin working immediately in pairs or trios (student choice).
- Students sit at tables in groups of five desks. The table arrangements facilitate small discussions.

Record of Evidence

Cluster 3: Classroom Management

Evidence (cont'd.)

- Students move quickly and quietly from small group interactions to whole class discussion. They are free to work standing or sitting.
- Students keep their noise level at a reasonable level for all to work. One male student in the navy turtleneck shirt is observed holding his ears during the neighbor discussion time. His ears are red, so holding them could have been for another reason other than the noise level.
- Directions appear to be clearly explained. A few students ask the teacher individual questions about their work, but it is not evident that the same question is being asked by multiple students, which might indicate some lack of clarity in directions.
- Students understand and comply with the established standards of conduct. No misbehavior is observed during this lesson. There is one student who the teacher speaks with multiple times about putting some of his thoughts on paper, but during the time on camera, he is not seen recording any information relative to the first part of the lesson's assignment. He is not in the classroom for the poster paper activity.

Interpretation

- It is not known whether the students had an active part in creating the standards of conduct.

- The physical environment of the classroom appears to support the instructional goals and learning activities. It is arranged so that small discussions can be facilitated with the table arrangements.

- Routines and procedures are clear and carried out efficiently by teacher and students with little loss of instructional time. Students move quickly and quietly from small group interactions to whole class discussion and are free to work standing or sitting .

- Students take an active role in the smooth operation by keeping their noise level at a reasonable level for all to work (with perhaps the exception of the one male student in the navy turtleneck shirt who was holding his ears).

Record of Evidence

Cluster 4: Student Intellectual Engagement

Guiding Questions

- *To what extent are students intellectually engaged in a classroom of high intellectual energy?*

- *What is the nature of what students are doing?*

- *Are they being challenged to think and make connections through both the instructional activities and the questions explored?*

- *Do the teacher's explanations of content correctly model academic language and invite intellectual work by students?*

- *Are students asked to explain their thinking, to construct logical arguments citing evidence, and to question the thinking of others?*

- *Are the instructional strategies used by the teacher suitable to the discipline, and to what extent do they promote student agency in the learning of challenging content?*

Evidence

- Students are challenged to think and make connections in the activities and questions explored.
- (16:39) Questions/discussions involve higher-order cognitive activity; students have time to develop their ideas and productive habits of mind.
- T: What do you call reading between the lines? Most of students respond in unison: Inference.
- T: What vocabulary was new, familiar, or unusual? Teacher calls student by name. S: Penicillin.
- T: How do you pronounce the word?
- T: What other words? S: Lysosome.
- T: What other words? S: Inoculate.
- T: Why do you think the author used words such as inoculates, vaccine, immune? Why does the author keep using those words over and over instead of varying their word choice?"
- (18:08) Some students raise their hands.
- T: How important are those words to these two articles?
- The teacher's explanation of content correctly models academic language and invites intellectual work by students. She shares a model for the poster paper activity prior to asking students to complete their own. Similarities and differences are shared, as are the expectations about vocabulary ("not dictionary definitions") and "the big idea" summary. Five differences are noted as required, but the teacher says she did the assignment herself and was able to come up with ten. She then challenges her students to themselves go beyond the minimum requirement.
- (21:57) Teacher puts example of graphic organizer on the board. T: Everyone is going to get a large piece of paper. The chart is divided into three horizontal sections with the top and bottom sections divided into half.
- Sections are labeled with the two articles.

Record of Evidence

Cluster 4: Student Intellectual Engagement

Evidence (cont'd.)

- Teacher brings students into the directions. T: What organizer do we typically use for similarities and differences?
- Students raise their hands.
- S: Venn Diagram.
- T: Please do at least five ideas about how they are different. I will come around and check...then move on to Level 2.
- T: Prove your point. I did this myself. Raise your hand if you have used the article and provided evidence. I will move you down to Level 3.
- Teacher provides clear directions for Level 3 activity and brings students into directions.
- T: What "Big Idea" do these two articles have?
- Student asks question about using your own words, citing, and abbreviating.
- T: In writing, or picture, or descriptive phrase for the Big Ideas. She provides examples to students.
- T: When you finish Level 1, raise your hand. When you finish Level 2, raise your hand.
- (29:30) Students begin working in groups with materials and resources.
- Teacher circulates around the room, checking understanding of each individual student and of group thinking.
- All students participate in the lesson, individually creating and writing ideas on their chart. Students are asked to explain their thinking, and upon occasion, cite evidence from the text (students have both texts out during the poster paper activity). Students mainly just share answers to the displayed Venn diagram sample (note 5 differences and 5 similarities between the texts, note new vocabulary in words/pictures, and summarize the big idea being stressed).
- Behavior is noticeably on-task. Student work artifacts and lesson video document teaching strategies that are appropriate to the subject and grade level.
- (48:52) T: We will finish tomorrow (teacher provided 27 minutes for group work).
- Small group work ends and transitions into closure of the lesson.

Interpretation

- Teacher models open-ended questions.

- Individuals are seated in small table groups of five for discussion.

- The instructional strategies are suitable for the discipline and seem to support students in the learning of challenging content by the noticeable on-task behavior and the evidence of the student work artifacts.

Record of Evidence

Cluster 5:   Successful Learning by All Students
Guiding Questions

- *To what extent does the teacher ensure learning by all students?*

- *Does the teacher monitor student understanding through specifically designed questions or instructional techniques?*

- *To what extent do students monitor their own learning and provide respectful feedback to classmates?*

- *Does the teacher make modifications in presentations or learning activities where necessary, taking into account the degree of student learning?*

- *Has the teacher sought out other resources (including parents) to support students' learning?*

- *In reflection, is the teacher aware of the success of the lesson in reaching students?*

Evidence
- (21:35) T: I am going to come around and probe your group's thinking.
- (33:44) Teacher circulates around the room, using proximity (kneeling by student), checking understanding of individual students and group thinking.
- Teacher uses open-ended questions to check for student understanding. Teacher also provides respectful, positive feedback to individuals throughout the lesson. Teacher reviews each student's work. If teacher approves student's work, teacher tells them to move on to Level 2.
- (39:43) T: Do you want me to give you a check? S: Yes.
- Teacher reviews student's work. T: Very observant. OK, you are good to go. Student begins immediately working on Level 2.
- (41:16) T: Anyone else need a check? Let me know, as you can move onto Level 2.
- Students raise thumb for a check.
- (41:48) T: The cliffhanger, what came out of it? Lots of choices.
- Student responds and teacher nods head.
- (42:52) T: I think it is really fascinating that as you are working on the differences portion, many of you and your neighbors right beside you are coming up with very different ideas, which is awesome. Very, very cool. You will be sharing these, so be sure that you are able to share your thinking.
- (46:06) T: Could you be more specific? What in science?" S: OK.
- T: Thank You. Student continues to work on Level 1.
- Some students are monitoring their own learning.
- There is not observable evidence of students providing respectful feedback to their classmates.

Record of Evidence

Cluster 5:   Successful Learning by All Students

Evidence (cont'd.)

- (48:49) T: We will probably need to finish tomorrow. I am seeing a lot of wonderful thinking.
- Teacher uses open-ended questions to check for student understanding as closure to activity. Teacher also provides respectful, positive feedback to individuals throughout the closure.
- Teacher asks questions while students are finishing work.
- T: What's the difference between bacteria and virus? Student responds.
- T: Which is easier to cure? S: Bacteria. T: Right.
- (51:33) T: How do you think accidents can be useful in science? Half of the students raise their hands.
- T: Thumbs up if you got to the similarity portion? Only about 10 students are seen to raise their thumbs.

Interpretation

- The teacher monitors student learning by checking in with individuals and small groups.

- Parents are not observed as additional resources for the lesson.

- The teacher's record keeping is not observed in the lesson video or artifacts.

- There is no evidence of the teacher's reflection about how the lesson could be improved.

- The Lesson Plan Reflection section outlines all 3 Core Action Indicators that will be visible in the lesson.

- It is not clear how the culminating poster paper activity is going to be assessed. Is there a rubric to use?

Record of Evidence

Cluster 6:   Professionalism

Guiding Questions

- *To what extent does the teacher engage with the professional community (within the school and beyond) and demonstrate a commitment to ongoing professional learning?*

- *Does the teacher collaborate productively with colleagues and contribute to the life of the school?*

- *Does the teacher engage in professional learning and take a leadership role in the school to promote the welfare of students?*

Evidence

No evidence of Cluster 6 is present in this Instructional Set.

FFT Clusters Study Guide: Set 6 (ELA 5)

**Looking at Teaching Through
the Lens of the FFT Clusters**

A Study Guide for
Teacher
Learning Communities

Teacher: Torney
Subject: Math
Grade: K
Topic: Composing Numbers

Welcome to the Study Guide for the Torney Math Instructional Set, a collection of artifacts and videos for an instructional lesson. This Study Guide provides information and instructions on how to examine teaching and learning through the lens of the Framework for Teaching (FFT) Clusters. In order to complete the steps in this Guide, you will need access to the teacher's planning documents, the lesson video, and the teacher commentary video (http://www.danielsongroup.org/study-guides/). Steps 1–5 of this Study Guide focus on examining the Instructional Set and can be done by an individual. Step 6 is a group activity and focuses on sharing results of the analysis and applications of learning.

Step 1 - Lesson Overview

Read the background information of the lesson provided below.

Students use a replica of a ten of hearts playing card in this lesson to discover the various ways to decompose the number ten.

The lesson begins with the teacher sharing two samples of student work from a previous lesson. In these samples, two students arrive at the same equation, $3 + 4 = 7$, although they have each circled a group of three hearts and a group of four hearts in different locations on a seven of hearts playing card. The discussion around the past assignment sets the stage for the new learning. Using a ten of hearts playing card, the teacher introduces two ways of decomposing the number 10 that both yield the equation $10 = 8 + 2$. Students are asked to individually notice, and then discuss what is similar and different about the two ways of decomposing 10. The teacher uses "equity sticks" to randomly call on students to share what they discussed with their partner.

Students are invited throughout the lesson to share their own thinking and/or to restate an explanation they heard from a peer. The teacher frequently follows-up a student's response with the question, "How do you know?" as a means to get students to justify their thinking. Based on their peer discussions and teacher prompting, the students recognize that there are multiple representations of the equation 10 = 8 + 2.

The teacher reviews the task directions, and expectations for respectful agreement and disagreement during peer conversations, before sending students to their tables for small group work. Students go to their tables with a marker and a replica of the ten of hearts card. They seek to determine other ways to represent the number ten, first by circling different combinations of groups of hearts that equal the number ten, and then by writing the equation that matches their representation. Once students have completed one card, they go to a bin to retrieve additional cards to show other combinations of numbers that add up to ten.

The teacher brings the students back together on the rug at the close of the lesson to share their learning. Students bring their "cards" with all their different representations and equations, and share them with a shoulder partner. The lesson ends with the teacher showing two samples of student work from the lesson. These samples show two ways of decomposing ten. Students are once again invited to share what is the same and what is different about the work, as well as anything else they notice.

Step 2 - Preparation and Questions

- *Read the teacher's lesson plan and jot down things you expect to see and what you want to look for in the video of the lesson.*

- *Write down any questions or comments you have about the lesson plan.*

Step 3 – Viewing the Classroom Video

- *View the complete video, noting those things you expected to see based on the lesson plan. Also note what was missing based on your expectations from the lesson plan. Jot down significant behaviors by the teacher and students pertinent to the FFT Clusters.*

Step 4 – Selected Highlights of the Lesson Video

Read the highlights of the lesson provided below. Note those matching your highlights of the lesson. For each set of statements, determine the FFT Cluster that is best related to the behaviors presented.

> A. *The teacher begins and ends the lesson with work completed by students in the classroom. By doing so, the teacher honors the thinking of the students in the classroom and reinforces the notion that the students in this class are part of a community of learners that make valuable contributions to their own learning and to the learning of their peers. (Cluster ___)*

B. The teacher encourages positive, respectful relationships among students. The teacher models his expectations by frequently using the word "please" when requesting something of students. He also uses the word "friend" when referring to students in the classroom. At one point in the lesson, he says to the class, "Thank you for letting your friend have her thinking time." When a student is talking he tells the class, "Let's show listening and respect... turn around toward our friend. Turn our eyes toward Isabella." (Cluster ___)

C. Students share and justify their thinking to the teacher and to their classmates. Throughout the lesson, the teacher emphasizes the thinking required to build conceptual understanding. The teacher asks a student "How do you know?" on at least three occasions during the lesson. Students then count the number of hearts in a particular group to "prove" or "double check" their answers. Before sharing with a classmate, students are given several seconds for individual think time. The teacher tells one student, "Mr. Torney doesn't care about you finding eight different ways...interested in you doing smart math." (Cluster ___)

D. The transitions to get students from one activity to the next are smooth and efficient. As the students prepare to leave the carpet, the teacher tells them to get a card after he gives them a marker. The teacher tells students to "touch their shoulders" and "touch the air" as a means of getting everyone's attention when they are engaged in small group work. The teacher asks his "mathematicians" to "freeze," then tells them to cap their markers before heading back to the carpet. (Cluster ___)

E. The teacher monitors student learning in different ways throughout the lesson. The teacher uses equity sticks to randomly select students to respond to his questions during the time that the students are seated on the rug as a whole group. He also asks students to repeat what they heard someone else say in response to a question. The *teacher moves to individual tables while students are engaged in small group conversations, <u>asking probing questions about</u> the solutions that students are illustrating. (Cluster ___).*

F. *Charts are posted around the room to reinforce expected student behavior and interactions. The teacher points out the chart that demonstrates how to respectfully disagree or agree with a peer before students go back to their tables to work on determining different ways to decompose 10. There are also charts that show expectations for active listening, and what to do when students are told to "freeze" in preparation for a transition. (Cluster ___)*

Step 5 – Viewing the Teacher Commentary

Watch the video of the teacher's commentary about the lesson and jot down any questions or comments you have about the commentary. Read the highlights below and identify the related FFT Cluster.

The teacher provides an extensive commentary in which he shares:

- the rationale for the lesson design

- the connections to the Common Core State Standards (CCSS) and the Core Actions

- reflections on how he would improve the lesson if he had an opportunity to teach the lesson again.

CCSS content standard K.OA.A3 that focuses on Operations and Algebraic Thinking is a driving force for this lesson. Specifically, students in this lesson are expected to be able to "decompose numbers less than or equal to ten into pairs in more than one way, e.g., by using objects or drawings, and record each decomposition by a drawing or equation." The teacher states that the lesson is a kindergarten standard that has no exact correlation in subsequent grades, but has implications for students' understanding of future math concepts. The lesson was designed to also exemplify Core Action 3 that acknowledges the need to establish a classroom community in which students are comfortable sharing their thinking.

A. The teacher designs the lesson so that students will be required to do most of the thinking without benefit of a standard direct instruction model in which the teacher models the behavior or skill and then has students go back to their tables and simply repeat what he did. Instead, the teacher designs the lesson so that students will have to grapple with the content and construct their own meaning based upon their work and their interactions with peers. (Cluster ___)

B. The teacher states in his reflection that he successfully orchestrated multiple conversations in the lesson in which students talked to each other about their thinking. As he looked around the room during small group work, he was pleased to see that all students in the class were interested in sharing their thinking, and incorporated precise mathematical language. (Cluster ___)

C. The teacher notices as he reviewed student work after the lesson that every student was able to decompose 10 in at least two different ways. He is pleased that students did not merely copy the example that he presented to them in the beginning that showed one decomposition to be $10 = 8 + 2$. Instead, he found that $5 + 5$ was the most frequent way that students decomposed 10, which leads him to believe that students were really using their own work and conversations with their peers to construct meaning. (Cluster ___)

Step 6 – Questions, Applications, and Discussion

The purpose of this step is to prompt your analysis and reflection of the Instructional Set and to have you think about applications to your own practice.

1. **Teaching and Learning Related to the FFT Clusters**

The purpose of the activity is to increase your understanding of the relationship between the highlights of the Instructional Set and the FFT Clusters. Your identification of an FFT Cluster for each of the highlights is compared to the Cluster identified by the master coders. The Answer Key is located at the end of the activities. You have options on how to complete the comparison. Determine what might work best for your group's learning. Options include, but are not limited to the following.

- Look at the first set of highlights. Take a poll of what each group member identified as the related FFT Cluster. If all members said the same FFT Cluster, have one or two members say why. Compare the group's response to the answer sheet. Repeat for the remainder of the highlights.

OR

- Have each member take one or two highlights. State the correct answer for each one, and a reason why the highlight demonstrates that FFT Cluster. The member will facilitate a discussion if others had different responses, with the goal of having all understand the justification of the correct answer.

OR

- Have members check their own responses to all the highlights. If there are any incorrect answers, then the member selects one highlight and leads a discussion with the group to learn why others think the highlight matches the correct FFT Cluster.

OR

- Determine your own process to check and discuss the match between highlights and the FFT Clusters.

2. **Analysis and Reflection of the Instructional Set**

The purpose of this activity is for you to analyze and reflect on what you saw and heard in the artifacts and videos, to share your analysis with your peers, and to discuss some of the questions or comments you noted. Review the notes, comments, and questions you recorded when you examined the Instructional Set.

- Identify a key teaching and learning attribute demonstrated in the Instructional Set that was effective and state why you think it worked well.

- Identify a different attribute and provide ideas about how it could be enhanced or improved.

- Share your statements with your group and have your peers react to and build upon your analysis and ideas.

Sample statements:

The teacher is purposeful in designing a lesson that invites students to share their thinking with their peers, both while they are under his supervision and while they work in small groups. When the students work with the teacher on the rug, he prompts them with the language that they should use when speaking to their peers. Students are able to use this language to explain their thinking as long as they are with the teacher and can respond to his prompts. It appears that the level of explanation of thinking among students while they are working in their groups is inconsistent, and not always on the same level as when they were sitting on the rug as a whole group. For example, when the teacher sits at some of the tables, he has to invite students to join the conversation about a tablemate's work. The teacher has to stop the group work at one point in the lesson to let the whole class know that it is OK to talk about their work with their peers. The teacher models what he wants conversations to sound like near the end of the lesson. Perhaps, in addition to the live modeling, the teacher could make video or audio recordings of the students using the language and prompts that he is expecting. Student self-assessment that includes the quality of feedback might be helpful as well.

Additional ideas for statements:

- Differentiation of tasks to meet the needs of individual students

- Clarification of the final product expected from students (e.g. showing 10 as the sum 8 + 2, circling different configurations of the hearts on the card, and/or showing 10 as the sum of different sets of numbers 5 + 5, 6 + 4, etc.)

- Incorporation of true group tasks and group thinking into future lessons

3. **Notice, Learn, and Apply**
The purpose of this activity is for you to reflect on what you learned from your analysis of the Instructional Set and to determine how you will apply it to your teaching.

- Complete the statements:
  "I noticed _____."
  (Insert one thing you noticed about the teacher or students.)

  "And I learned _____."
  (State what you learned related to what you noticed.)

  "I will apply what I learned by _____."
  (Provide example of how you will use what you learned in your own context.)

- Share your statements with your group. Have others react and add how they might apply what you noticed to their own teaching context.

Sample statement:

- I noticed that students did not consistently share their thinking in the absence of teacher prompting.

- I learned that students need ongoing practice and multiple opportunities to use Accountable Talk that encourages students to speak to each other in respectful ways. More importantly, if students do not learn to use this skill on their own, they will miss valuable opportunities to deepen their understanding by sharpening their metacognitive skills.

- I will apply what I learned by looking for opportunities to reinforce this skill throughout the day, everyday, and will deliberately point out instances when students model this skill without teacher prompting.

Study Guide for Teachers Answer Key

Highlights from the Lesson Video (Step 4)

A. The teacher begins and ends the lesson with work completed by students in the classroom. By doing so, the teacher honors the thinking of the students in the classroom and reinforces the notion that the students in this class are part of a community of learners that make valuable contributions to their own learning and to the learning of their peers. (Cluster 2 Safe, Respectful, Supportive, and Challenging Learning Environment)

B. The teacher encourages positive, respectful relationships among students. The teacher models his expectations by frequently using the word "please" when requesting something of students. He also uses the word "friend" when referring to students in the classroom. At one point in the lesson, he says to the class, "Thank you for letting your friend have her thinking time." When a student is talking he tells the class, "Let's show listening and respect... turn around toward our friend. Turn our eyes toward Isabella." (Cluster 2 Safe, Respectful, Supportive, and Challenging Learning Environment)

C. Students share and justify their thinking to the teacher and to their classmates. Throughout the lesson, the teacher emphasizes the thinking required to build conceptual understanding. The teacher asks a student "How do you know?" on at least three occasions during the lesson. Students then count the number of hearts in a particular group to "prove" or "double check" their answers. Before sharing with a classmate, students are given several seconds for individual think time. The teacher tells one student, "Mr. Torney doesn't care about you finding eight different ways... interested in you doing smart math." (Cluster 4 Student Intellectual Engagement)

D. The transitions to get students from one activity to the next are smooth and efficient. As the students prepare to leave the carpet, the teacher tells them to get a card after he gives them a marker. The teacher tells students to "touch their shoulders" and "touch the air" as a means of getting everyone's attention when they are engaged in small group work. The teacher asks his "mathematicians" to "freeze," then tells them to cap their markers before heading back to the carpet. (Cluster 3 Classroom Management)

E. The teacher monitors student learning in different ways throughout the lesson. The teacher uses equity sticks to randomly select students to respond to his questions during the time that the students are seated on the rug as a whole group. He also asks students to repeat what they heard someone else say in response to a question. The teacher moves to individual tables while students are engaged in small group conversations, asking probing questions about the solutions that students are illustrating. (Cluster 5 Successful Learning by All Students)

FFT Clusters Study Guide: Set 6 (Math K)

Study Guide for Teachers Answer Key

Highlights from the Lesson Video (Step 4—cont'd.)

F. Charts are posted around the room to reinforce expected student behavior and interactions. The teacher points out the chart that demonstrates how to respectfully disagree or agree with a peer before students go back to their tables to work on determining different ways to decompose 10. There are also charts that show expectations for active listening, and what to do when students are told to "freeze" in preparation for a transition. (Cluster 3 Classroom Management)

Study Guide for Teachers Answer Key

Highlights from the Teacher Commentary (Step 5)

A. The teacher designs the lesson so that students will be required to do most of the thinking without benefit of a standard direct instruction model in which the teacher models the behavior or skill and then has students go back to their tables and simply repeat what he did. Instead, the teacher designs the lesson so that students will have to grapple with the content and construct their own meaning based upon their work and their interactions with peers. (Cluster 1 Clarity of Instructional Purpose and Accuracy of Content)

B. The teacher states in his reflection that he successfully orchestrated multiple conversations in the lesson in which students talked to each other about their thinking. As he looked around the room during small group work, he was pleased to see that all students in the class were interested in sharing their thinking, and incorporated precise mathematical language. (Cluster 1 Clarity of Instructional Purpose and Accuracy of Content)

C. The teacher notices that every student was able to decompose 10 in at least two different ways as he reviewed student work after the lesson. He is pleased that students did not merely copy the example that he presented to them in the beginning that showed one decomposition to be 10 = 8 + 2. Instead, he found that 5 +5 was the most frequent way that students decomposed 10, which leads him to believe that students were really using their own work and conversations with their peers to construct meaning. (Cluster 5 Successful Learning by All Students)

**Looking at Teaching Through
the Lens of the FFT Clusters**

A Study Guide for
Instructional Coach
Learning Communities

Teacher: Torney
Subject: Math
Grade: K
Topic: Composing Numbers

Welcome to the Study Guide for the Torney Math Instructional Set, a collection of artifacts and videos for an instructional lesson. This Study Guide provides information and instructions on how to examine teaching and learning through the lens of the Framework for Teaching (FFT) Clusters. In order to complete the steps in this Guide, you will need access to the teacher's planning documents, the lesson video, and the teacher commentary video (http://www.danielsongroup.org/study-guides/). Steps 1–5 of this Study Guide focus on examining the Instructional Set and can be done by an individual. Step 6 is a group activity and focuses on sharing results of the analysis and applications of learning.

Step 1 - Lesson Overview

Read the background information of the lesson provided below.

Students use a replica of a ten of hearts playing card in this lesson to discover the various ways to decompose the number ten.

The lesson begins with the teacher sharing two samples of student work from a previous lesson. In these samples, two students arrive at the same equation, $3 + 4 = 7$, although they have each circled a group of three hearts and a group of four hearts in different locations on a seven of hearts playing card. The discussion around the past assignment sets the stage for the new learning. Using a ten of hearts playing card, the teacher introduces two ways of decomposing the number 10 that both yield the equation $10 = 8 + 2$. Students are asked to individually notice, and then discuss what is similar and different about the two ways of decomposing 10. The teacher uses "equity sticks" to randomly call on students to share what they discussed with their partner.

Students are invited throughout the lesson to share their own thinking and/or to restate an explanation they heard from a peer. The teacher frequently follows-up a student's response with the question, "How do you know?" as a means to get students to justify their thinking. Based on their peer discussions and teacher prompting, the students recognize that there are multiple representations of the equation $10 = 8 + 2$.

The teacher reviews the task directions, and expectations for respectful agreement and disagreement during peer conversations, before sending students to their tables for small group work. Students go to their tables with a marker and a replica of the ten of hearts card. They seek to determine other ways to represent the number ten, first by circling different combinations of groups of hearts that equal the number ten, and then by writing the equation that matches their representation. Once students have completed one card, they go to a bin to retrieve additional cards to show other combinations of numbers that add up to ten.

The teacher brings the students back together on the rug at the close of the lesson to share their learning. Students bring their "cards" with all their different representations and equations, and share them with a shoulder partner. The lesson ends with the teacher showing two samples of student work from the lesson. These samples show two ways of decomposing ten. Students are once again invited to share what is the same and what is different about the work, as well as anything else they notice.

Step 2 - Preparation and Questions

- *Read the teacher's lesson plan and jot down things you expect to see and what you want to look for in the video of the lesson.*

- *Write down any questions or comments you have about the lesson plan.*

Step 3 – Viewing the Classroom Video

- *View the complete video, noting those things you expected to see based on the lesson plan. Also note what was missing based on your expectations from the lesson plan. Jot down significant behaviors by the teacher and students pertinent to the FFT Clusters.*

Step 4 – Selected Highlights of the Lesson Video

Read the highlights of the lesson provided below. Note those matching your highlights of the lesson. For each set of statements, determine the FFT Cluster that is best related to the behaviors presented.

> A. *The teacher begins and ends the lesson with work completed by students in the classroom. By doing so, the teacher honors the thinking of the students in the classroom and reinforces the notion that the students in this class are part of a community of learners that make valuable contributions to their own learning and to the learning of their peers. (Cluster ____)*

B. *The teacher encourages positive, respectful relationships among students. The teacher models his expectations by frequently using the word "please" when requesting something of students. He also uses the word "friend" when referring to students in the classroom. At one point in the lesson, he says to the class, "Thank you for letting your friend have her thinking time." When a student is talking he tells the class, "Let's show listening and respect... turn around toward our friend. Turn our eyes toward Isabella." (Cluster ___)*

C. *Students share and justify their thinking to the teacher and to their classmates. Throughout the lesson, the teacher emphasizes the thinking required to build conceptual understanding. The teacher asks a student "How do you know?" on at least three occasions during the lesson. Students then count the number of hearts in a particular group to "prove" or "double check" their answers. Before sharing with a classmate, students are given several seconds for individual think time. The teacher tells one student, "Mr. Torney doesn't care about you finding eight different ways...interested in you doing smart math." (Cluster ___)*

D. *The transitions to get students from one activity to the next are smooth and efficient. As the students prepare to leave the carpet, the teacher tells them to get a card after he gives them a marker. The teacher tells students to "touch their shoulders" and "touch the air" as a means of getting everyone's attention when they are engaged in small group work. The teacher asks his "mathematicians" to "freeze," then tells them to cap their markers before heading back to the carpet. (Cluster ___)*

E. *The teacher monitors student learning in different ways throughout the lesson. The teacher uses equity sticks to randomly select students to respond to his questions during the time that the students are seated on the rug as a whole group. He also asks students to repeat what they heard someone else say in response to a question. The teacher moves to individual tables while students are en-*

gaged in small group conversations, asking probing questions about the solutions that students are illustrating. (Cluster ___)

F. *Charts are posted around the room to reinforce expected student behavior and interactions. The teacher points out the chart that demonstrates how to respectfully disagree or agree with a peer before students go back to their tables to work on determining different ways to decompose 10. There are also charts that show expectations for active listening, and what to do when students are told to "freeze" in preparation for a transition. (Cluster ___)*

Step 5 – Viewing the Teacher Commentary

Watch the video of the teacher's commentary about the lesson and jot down any questions or comments you have about the commentary. Read the highlights below and identify the related FFT Cluster.

The teacher provides an extensive commentary in which he shares:

- the rationale for the lesson design

- the connections to the Common Core State Standards (CCSS) and the Core Actions

- reflections on how he would improve the lesson if he had an opportunity to teach the lesson again.

CCSS content standard K.OA.A3 that focuses on Operations and Algebraic Thinking is a driving force for this lesson. Specifically, students in this lesson are expected to be able to "decompose numbers less than or equal to ten into pairs in more than one way, e.g., by using objects or drawings, and record each decomposition by a drawing or equation." The teacher states that the lesson is a kindergarten standard that has no exact correlation in subsequent grades, but has implications for students' understanding of future math concepts. The lesson was designed to also exemplify Core Action 3 that acknowledges the need to establish a classroom community in which students are comfortable sharing their thinking.

A. The teacher designs the lesson so that students will be required to do most of the thinking without benefit of a standard direct instruction model in which the teacher models the behavior or skill and then has students go back to their tables and simply repeat what he did. Instead, the teacher designs the lesson so that students will have to grapple with the content and construct their own meaning based upon their work and their interactions with peers. (Cluster ___)

B. The teacher states in his reflection that he successfully orchestrated multiple conversations in the lesson in which students talked to each other about their thinking. As he looked around the room during small group work, he was pleased to see that all students in the class were interested in sharing their thinking, and incorporated precise mathematical language. (Cluster ___)

C. The teacher notices as he reviewed student work after the lesson that every student was able to decompose 10 in at least two different ways. He is pleased that students did not merely copy the example that he presented to them in the beginning that showed one decomposition to be 10 = 8 + 2. Instead, he found that 5 +5 was the most frequent way that students decomposed 10, which leads him to believe that students were really using their own work and conversations with their peers to construct meaning. (Cluster ___)

Step 6 – Questions, Applications, and Discussion

The purpose of this step is to prompt your analysis and reflection of the Instructional Set and to have you think about applications to your own practice.

1. **Teaching and Learning Related to the FFT Clusters**

The purpose of the activity is to increase your understanding of the relationship between the highlights of the Instructional Set and the FFT Clusters. Your identification of an FFT Cluster for each of the highlights is compared to the Cluster identified by the master coders. The Answer Key is located at the end of the activities. You have options on how to complete the comparison. Determine what might work best for your group's learning. Options include, but are not limited to the following.

- Look at the first set of highlights. Take a poll of what each group member identified as the related FFT Cluster. If all members said the same FFT Cluster, then have one or two members say why. Compare the group's response to the answer sheet. Repeat for the remainder of the sets of highlights.

OR

- Have each member take one or two sets of highlights and be the discussant for them. The discussant will state the correct answer and state a reason why the statements in the set demonstrate the FFT Cluster. The discussant will facilitate a discussion if members had different responses with the goal of all understanding the justification of the correct answer.

OR

- Have members check their own responses to all the sets of highlights. If there are any incorrect answers, then the member selects one set and leads a discussion with the group to learn why others think the highlights match the correct FFT Cluster.

OR

- Determine your own process to check and discuss the match between highlights and the FFT Clusters.

2. **Analysis and Reflection of the Instructional Set**

The purpose of this activity is for you to analyze and reflect on what you saw and heard in the artifacts and videos and to discuss some of the questions or comments you noted. One element of a professional conversation is asking questions to ascertain more information about a teacher's thinking and the behaviors of both students and teacher. This activity allows you and your peers to practice preparing such questions. Your peers can comment on whether your questions are appropriate and will obtain useful information without making the featured teacher feel uneasy or criticized.

The second part of this activity focuses on helping teachers move their practice forward. Please note that having you prepare for and model an entire conversation about the lesson with the featured teacher is not the purpose of this activity as written. Your group can modify or replace the activity to meet your group's needs

- Review the notes, comments, and questions you recorded when you examined the Instructional Set. Pretend you have the opportunity to ask the teacher some questions to get additional information about the strategies used or decisions made for this Instructional Set.

- Share with your group just the questions you would use with the teacher to elicit additional information. Have your peers comment about your questions and add other questions they had about the same event.

- Share with others in your group what you would do to prompt the teacher's thinking and actions to enhance his/her practice. Take turns sharing and discussing the prompts.

Sample A, Part I:

You used the "equity sticks" on several occasions during your lesson as a means to call on students to share their responses with the class. This appeared to be a familiar routine in your class, as evidenced by the students immediately reading the name on the stick each time you pulled a stick from the can. This randomness in calling on students helps students to recognize that you expect all students to be ready to reply if their names are selected. I noticed that after you pulled a student's name from the can, you placed in on the ledge of the whiteboard. At other times, you called on student volunteers. Would you tell me how you decide which method to use to call on students? Would you tell me a little more about your method of using the sticks and how your students have benefited from the use of this routine in your instruction? When, during the course of a lesson, is a student's stick returned to the can after they have been called upon once?

Sample A, Part II:

One of the benefits of using the "equity sticks" is that it keeps all students alert. In other words, all students are fair game for any question that the teacher asks of the class. What do you think might happen if you return each student's stick immediately after they are called on? In what ways does this align with a formative use of this tool? How might your students react to the same student being called upon in the same lesson? I observed another class of kindergarteners where the teacher kept her equity sticks in an inside/outside can configuration. In other words, for some lessons, when she called on a student, she placed their stick into the outside can. Students were not aware that there were two cans, so to them it appeared that all names would go back into the same pile after they were called upon. This gave the teacher a little more control for those instances when she wanted to get more voices in the room. Given the students that you teach and your own teaching style, how might the inside/outside can configuration work for you and your students?

Sample B, Part I:

You were consistent in incorporating student work as a centerpiece in your lesson by sharing student work from a previous lesson at the beginning of the lesson and having those students share their mathematical thinking with the rest of the class. You then circled back to another example of student work at the end of the class and put it up for group discussion. In both lessons, you used playing cards as the model that students would use to explain their thinking. Would you share a little more about your selection of the playing card as the tool that students use to draw their models and to explain their thinking?

Sample B, Part II:

One of the ways that students deepen their understanding of a concept is by generalizing their learning from one situation to the next. The playing card is a convenient tool to use when helping students understand the decomposition of numbers from one to ten. What other models besides a playing card could you use to check students' understanding of the concept of decomposition of ten, either in this lesson or in an extension or follow-up to this lesson? As you think about the students in your class, what would you anticipate might happen if students in your class were asked to generalize their learning using another model?

3. **Notice, Learn, and Apply**

The purpose of this activity is for you to reflect on what you learned from your analysis of the Instructional Set and to determine how you will apply it to your teaching.

- Complete the statements:
  "I noticed _____."
  (Insert one thing you noticed about the teacher or students.)

  "And I learned _____."
  (State what you learned related to what you noticed.)

  "I will apply what I learned by _____."
  (Provide example of how you will use what you learned in your own context.)

- Share your statements with your group. Have others react and add how they might apply what you noticed to their own coaching context.

Sample statements:

- I noticed that all students were able to complete the task. As a teacher, I might assume that all students were beginning to understand the concept that I was teaching.

- I learned that in order for students to demonstrate their understanding at high levels, they need to be able to apply their learning to multiple settings.

- As I work with teachers, I will emphasize the need to assess student learning in multiple ways using multiple models. This will give the teacher a clearer picture of the level of student understanding and whether or not students have really gained the prerequisite knowledge and skills necessary to move on to the exploration of related topics and concepts. As I am watching the video with teachers that I coach, we will look for possible missed opportunities to assess individual student learning.

Study Guide for Instructional Coaches Answer Key
Highlights from the Lesson Video (Step 4)

A. The teacher begins and ends the lesson with work completed by students in the classroom. By doing so, the teacher honors the thinking of the students in the classroom and reinforces the notion that the students in this class are part of a community of learners that make valuable contributions to their own learning and to the learning of their peers. (Cluster 2 Safe, Respectful, Supportive, and Challenging Learning Environment)

B. The teacher encourages positive, respectful relationships among students. The teacher models his expectations by frequently using the word "please" when requesting something of students. He also uses the word "friend" when referring to students in the classroom. At one point in the lesson, he says to the class, "Thank you for letting your friend have her thinking time." When a student is talking he tells the class, "Let's show listening and respect… turn around toward our friend. Turn our eyes toward Isabella." (Cluster 2 Safe, Respectful, Supportive, and Challenging Learning Environment)

C. Students share and justify their thinking to the teacher and to their classmates. Throughout the lesson, the teacher emphasizes the thinking required to build conceptual understanding. The teacher asks a student "How do you know?" on at least three occasions during the lesson. Students then count the number of hearts in a particular group to "prove" or "double check" their answers. Before sharing with a classmate, students are given several seconds for individual think time. The teacher tells one student, "Mr. Torney doesn't care about you finding eight different ways… interested in you doing smart math." (Cluster 4 Student Intellectual Engagement)

D. The transitions to get students from one activity to the next are smooth and efficient. As the students prepare to leave the carpet, the teacher tells them to get a card after he gives them a marker. The teacher tells students to "touch their shoulders" and "touch the air" as a means of getting everyone's attention when they are engaged in small group work. The teacher asks his "mathematicians" to "freeze," then tells them to cap their markers before heading back to the carpet. (Cluster 3 Classroom Management)

E. The teacher monitors student learning in different ways throughout the lesson. The teacher uses equity sticks to randomly select students to respond to his questions during the time that the students are seated on the rug as a whole group. He also asks students to repeat what they heard someone else say in response to a question. The teacher moves to individual tables while students are engaged in small group conversations, asking probing questions about the solutions that students are illustrating. (Cluster 5 Successful Learning by All Students)

Study Guide for Instructional Coaches Answer Key
Highlights from the Lesson Video (Step 4—cont'd.)

F. Charts are posted around the room to reinforce expected student behavior and interactions. The teacher points out the chart that demonstrates how to respectfully disagree or agree with a peer before students go back to their tables to work on determining different ways to decompose 10. There are also charts that show expectations for active listening, and what to do when students are told to "freeze" in preparation for a transition. (Cluster 3 Classroom Management)

Study Guide for Instructional Coaches Answer Key
Highlights from the Teacher Commentary (Step 5)

A. The teacher designs the lesson so that students will be required to do most of the thinking without benefit of a standard direct instruction model in which the teacher models the behavior or skill and then has students go back to their tables and simply repeat what he did. Instead, the teacher designs the lesson so that students will have to grapple with the content and construct their own meaning based upon their work and their interactions with peers. (Cluster 1 Clarity of Instructional Purpose and Accuracy of Content)

B. The teacher states in his reflection that he successfully orchestrated multiple conversations in the lesson in which students talked to each other about their thinking. As he looked around the room during small group work, he was pleased to see that all students in the class were interested in sharing their thinking, and incorporated precise mathematical language. (Cluster 1 Clarity of Instructional Purpose and Accuracy of Content)

C. The teacher notices that every student was able to decompose 10 in at least two different ways as he reviewed student work after the lesson. He is pleased that students did not merely copy the example that he presented to them in the beginning that showed one decomposition to be $10 = 8 + 2$. Instead, he found that $5 + 5$ was the most frequent way that students decomposed 10, which leads him to believe that students were really using their own work and conversations with their peers to construct meaning. (Cluster 5 Successful Learning by All Students)

Record of Evidence

This Record of Evidence (ROE) contains key evidence aligned to the FFT Clusters. Interpretive statements about the evidence are also provided. The ROE was created by two master coders who recorded evidence and interpretation statements independently, reviewed each others' work, and arrived at a final composite version based on their professional conversations. This version was reviewed by a leader of the master coders. The ROE is included in this Study Guide so users can see what master coders identified as key evidence, and their interpretation of that evidence through the lens of the FFT Clusters. It is provided as an example of one type of analysis of an Instructional Set. The ROEs were created for professional development rather than evaluative purposes. Users are cautioned about using them for teacher evaluation.

Rubric: Generic

Grade: K

Subject: Math

Topic: Composing Numbers

Teacher description: Male

Record of Evidence

Cluster 1: Clarity of Instructional Purpose and Accuracy of Content

Guiding Questions

- *To what extent does the teacher demonstrate depth of important content knowledge and conduct the class with a clear and ambitious purpose, reflective of the standards for the discipline and appropriate to the students' levels of knowledge and skill?*

- *To what degree are the elements of a lesson (the sequence of topics, instructional strategies, and materials and resources) well designed and executed, and aligned with the purpose of the lesson?*

- *To what extent are they designed to engage students in high-level learning in the discipline?*

Evidence

Instructional Plan
- The teacher identifies two CCSS Math Standards that align with the lesson.
- Learning targets:
    - Students will be able to decompose numbers less than or equal to 10 into pairs in more than one way and record with a drawing or an equation.
    - Students will be able to find the number that makes 10 when added to any given number from 1-9.
- The teacher states that composing and decomposing numbers builds procedural skill and fluency in math.
- The teacher describes previous skills that students have been taught, including numbers to 10, counting to 100 by 1s and 10s, understanding numbers 11-19 as 10 ones and some ones, and 2-D and 3-D shapes.
- This lesson is designed to help students understand a special case of composing and decomposing numbers to make 10, in preparation for understanding the base 10 system.
- Lesson sequence:
    - Introducing
    - Exploring/Extending
    - Summarizing

Activities
- The teacher will show students sample work on decomposing numbers from the previous day. Students turn and talk and come to agreement that the work represents $10 = 9 + 1$. The teacher shows students 9 hearts and asks them how many more do they need to make 10. Have students think independently, share their thinking, and then write an equation. Have students explain the similarities to decomposing of numbers done earlier (same equation). Use second example if need-

Record of Evidence

Cluster 1: Clarity of Instructional Purpose and Accuracy of Content

Evidence (cont'd.)

ed. Students go back to tables and work on drawing other ways to make ten with other numbers and writing equations. Bring students back together to summarize.

Video

- The teacher reminds students at the beginning of the lesson that in the last lesson, they worked on decomposing numbers.
- The teacher tells student to ask him if he agrees or disagrees.
- T: Be careful I may call on you.
- The teacher says good morning to a student who comes in late.
- The teacher tells student to use the loud voice.
- T: I want us to remember this important group of math idea. As… said, in total or in all.
- The teacher tells student that he is showing persistence in drawing a heart.
- The teacher tells a student that he noticed that the student noticed something about the equation.
- The teacher holds up a card and tells students that when they go back to their tables, they will get a pack of cards, and will have to figure out how many hearts they need to make 10.
- The teacher holds up one set . T: There's a tricky one.
- The teacher pulls out packets with different number of hearts on the paper.
- T: Today, your job is to make 10. We are not decomposing.
- The teacher tells a student that he stuck with it. T: Nice work.
- T: Let's be an accurate counter.
- The teacher refers back to the mini-lesson at least 3 times when helping students at the tables.
- The teacher asks another student to repeat what Abilyn said.
- The teacher asks a student to repeat the explanation because he wants to be sure that he understands the student's mathematical thinking.
- A student looks at a peer's paper and tells him that he did not "X" out one of the hearts. T: Why is X-ing out one going to make 10? Prove to me that it is 10 and write your number sentence please.
- T: Your brains really grew today. We are going to finish this another day.

Record of Evidence

Cluster 1:   Clarity of Instructional Purpose and Accuracy of Content

Interpretation

- The teacher aligns the learning targets and activities with the Common Core State Standards (CCSS).

- The teacher explains how the lesson fits in with a sequence of instruction

- The teacher uses academic language (decomposing).

Record of Evidence

Cluster 2: Safe, Respectful, Supportive, and Challenging Learning Environment

Guiding Questions

- *To what extent do the interactions between teacher and students, and among students, demonstrate genuine caring and a safe, respectful, supportive, and also challenging learning environment?*

- *Do teachers convey high expectations for student learning and encourage hard work and perseverance? Is the environment safe for risk taking?*

- *Do students take pride in their work and demonstrate a commitment to mastering challenging content?*

Evidence

- The teacher asks a student to repeat her explanation because he wants to be sure that he understands her mathematical thinking.
- The teacher asks a student to repeat what his friend Abigail said, in her words or in his words.
- As the teacher pulls a stick, students read the name on the stick.
- The teacher tells a student that he is doing the right thing by putting his eyes on Evelyn as she explains her important idea. All students turn around to look at the speaker.
- The teacher explains to students that since they are mathematicians, they should ask their friends to "prove it" or "how do you know?"
- Student has difficulty making a heart, and the teacher acknowledges that student has been "experimenting" making hearts.
- A student interrupts when the teacher is working with a group. T: Wait a minute dear.
- The teacher sits on rug near a group of students as they share their thinking.
- The teacher takes out the original student work at the end of the lesson, and posts it for the class to see. T: Is that all right Maria?
- The teacher tells students that it can be scary when we are sick. T: Breathe in and out....
- T: Your brains really grew today.

Record of Evidence

Cluster 2:   Safe, Respectful, Supportive, and Challenging Learning Environment

---

Interpretation

- The teacher makes respectful connections with students.

- The teacher insists that students turn toward a speaker, and be quiet when a classmate is talking.

- The teacher demonstrates high regard for student thinking.

Record of Evidence

Cluster 3:   Classroom Management

Guiding Questions

- *Is the classroom well run and organized?*

- *Are classroom routines and procedures clear and carried out efficiently by both teacher and students with little loss of instructional time?*

- *To what extent do students themselves take an active role in their smooth operation?*

- *Are directions for activities clearly explained so that there is no confusion?*

- *Do students not only understand and comply with standards of conduct, but also play an active part in setting the tone for maintaining those standards?*

- *How does the physical environment support the learning activities?*

Evidence
- The students start the lesson sitting on the floor in rows, facing the teacher.
- T: Give me a "me-too" if you remember that. All students point to themselves.
- The teacher tells a student that he is doing the right thing by putting his eyes on Evelyn as she explains her important idea. All students turn around to look at the speaker.
- The teacher does a 3-2-1 to choose a classmate to come up to answer a question. The teacher tells students that when he calls their row, they can grab a packet and go back to their seats. As two students are working, the teacher goes to their table. Student gives an answer and partner says, "Can you prove it?"
- T: Derek, can you use your self-control?
- The teacher guides this student to his seat and helps him with his work. Student is having difficulty making a heart, and the teacher acknowledges that student has been "experimenting" with making hearts.
- A student comes to the teacher and says that he needs a paper. The teacher points to his hat and says, "Tell Derek."
- As students finish with one packet of work, they can be seen going to the front of room and getting another packet to work on.
- The teacher tells one student to make sure that he is learning from his friend Abigail.
- T: Check yourself in 1, check yourself in 2, check yourself in 3.
- The teacher says, "Turn this way please" three times, and all students turn to face the front and sit quietly looking at the teacher.
- The teacher tells a student to hold on for a second, and stops the lesson until all students are listening. He gives a thumbs up to a student, but then stops again and tells the "invited" student to go to his... (spider?).

Record of Evidence

Cluster 3:   Classroom Management

Interpretation

- Routines are in place that encourage students to participate when they are in a large group during the lesson.

- The teacher has routines in place that encourage students to manage their own behavior.

- There are established expectations for student behavior when they are sitting on the rug in a large group.

Record of Evidence

Cluster 4: Student Intellectual Engagement

Guiding Questions

- *To what extent are students intellectually engaged in a classroom of high intellectual energy?*

- *What is the nature of what students are doing?*

- *Are they being challenged to think and make connections through both the instructional activities and the questions explored?*

- *Do the teacher's explanations of content correctly model academic language and invite intellectual work by students?*

- *Are students asked to explain their thinking, to construct logical arguments citing evidence, and to question the thinking of others?*

- *Are the instructional strategies used by the teacher suitable to the discipline, and to what extent do they promote student agency in the learning of challenging content?*

Evidence

- The teacher shows students a copy of Maria's way and asks them what the numbers mean.
- Students are told to turn to their partners and tell them what they see.
- Students appeared to be talking to a partner.
- T (showing a 9 of hearts card): How many more hearts do I need to make ten? The teacher repeats the question three times and asks students to put their answer in their heads.
- The teacher repeats what a student said as he explained his answer. The teacher pulls manipulatives T: We are going to count to see if that makes 10.
- Student says that s/he learned how to make a ten from Maria's answer.
- The teacher tells students that he thinks this is an important math idea that will help them understand what they will be doing today.
- T: What did we learn today? Ss: We learned that 1 + 9 makes 10.
- The teacher halts student work to say that he heard a good idea.
- The teacher asks where is the group of 1 on Danielle's. T: She is showing some really good math thinking.
- The teacher tells students to double check by counting, to make sure that 1 + 9 is still 10. The teacher asks a student to ask his friends if he was ready to help us count. The teacher tells a student to use the same counting path so that he can be more accurate in his counting.
- Student gives an answer. T: I'm interested to see if that is right.
- The teacher tells students that although they are not decomposing, they can ask themselves how composing and decomposing are similar as they are working.
- The teacher explains to students that since they are mathematicians, they should ask their friends to "prove it" or "how do you know?"
- A student says that one of the problems is tricky. The teacher asks what is tricky about the problem.

Record of Evidence

Cluster 4: Student Intellectual Engagement

Evidence (cont'd.)

- The teacher asks Brandon if there is something similar about the two ways that he and his friend made 10. Teacher reminds students that they had talked about opposites and asks if there is something that is opposite.
- The teacher displays the work of two students.

Interpretation

- The learning tasks and questions require higher-order thinking.

- The focus is on student learning, and not on just completing a task.

- The teacher asks students to explain their thinking in partner and whole-group discussion.

- Students are encouraged to challenge fellow classmates to justify their thinking.

- Students are asked to make connections between today's learning and previous learning.

Record of Evidence

Cluster 5:   Successful Learning by All Students
Guiding Questions

- *To what extent does the teacher ensure learning by all students?*

- *Does the teacher monitor student understanding through specifically designed questions or instructional techniques?*

- *To what extent do students monitor their own learning and provide respectful feedback to classmates?*

- *Does the teacher make modifications in presentations or learning activities where necessary, taking into account the degree of student learning?*

- *Has the teacher sought out other resources (including parents) to support students' learning?*

- *In reflection, is the teacher aware of the success of the lesson in reaching students?*

Evidence

- The teacher pulls a stick and calls up a partner to explain what she said to her partner.
- Student is told to find a friend who can say more.
- The teacher asks student if he agrees with Abigail. T: Why? Can you explain that to us?
- T (after counting): What did we learn? S: We learned that the number is ten. The teacher points to each group of hearts to elicit that $1 + 9 = 10$.
- The teacher tells students that he has some math frames in case they need to check their work.
- He says that he will be walking around and conferencing with students as they are working.
- The teacher goes to one student to check in, and tells him that he is working on decomposing. He then asks student what they are working on today. S: Making 10. T: Do you need more hearts or less hearts to make 10.
- S: Five and three is not 10. T: How do you know? The student counts hearts on his page.
- T: We learned that 5 and 3 makes 8.
- The teacher moves to each table as students are working.
- T: How many hearts are in this group? What's your next step? Do it.
- The teacher asks a student what symbol means the same as.
- Student tells teacher that she has finished her work. The teacher asks if she has explained her thinking to someone else.

Record of Evidence

Cluster 5:   Successful Learning by All Students

Evidence (cont'd.)

- Student looks at peer's paper and tells him that he did not "X" out one of the hearts. T: Why is "X-ing" out one going to make 10? Prove to me that it is 10 and write your number sentence please.
- The teacher brings students back to rug with their papers after group work at tables. He asks for a volunteer to show how they made 10. Abilyn comes up to the document reader to share her thinking. The teacher asks another student to repeat what Abilyn said.
- The teacher takes out the original student work at the end of the lesson ("Is that all right Maria?"). T: I want you to find out what is similar and what is different about the work. The teacher partners up with one student. The teacher listens in.
- T: Do you agree? Why do you agree? Those groups are in different places. How do they still make 10?
- Closure discussion talks about what is similar and different from yesterday's experience.

Interpretation

- The teacher randomly calls on students to explain their thinking.

- The teacher monitors student learning throughout the lesson by visiting tables as students are working and asking them to explain their reasoning. The focus is on student learning and not just doing the work.

- Students are asked to explain why they agree or disagree with a classmate's response.

- The teacher asks students to demonstrate their learning in multiple ways: responding to questions, drawing, and writing a number sentence.

- The teacher encourages students to check their work.

- The teacher circles back to the original problem at the end of the lesson and asks students to explain their thinking. This step is also indicated in the lesson plan.

Record of Evidence

Cluster 6: Professionalism

Guiding Questions

- *To what extent does the teacher engage with the professional community (within the school and beyond) and demonstrate a commitment to ongoing professional learning?*

- *Does the teacher collaborate productively with colleagues and contribute to the life of the school?*

- *Does the teacher engage in professional learning and take a leadership role in the school to promote the welfare of students?*

Evidence

No evidence of Cluster 6 is present in this Instructional Set.

Appendix A: The FFT Clusters
Study Guide Series Team

Ron Anderson, EdD; OH. Danielson Group Consultant.

Dauna Easley, MEd; OH. University of Cincinnati supervisor for student teachers.

Nancy Flickinger, MEd; OH. National Board Certified (AYA/ELA), Teaching Professions Academy Instructor.

Linda Goodwin, MEd; AR. Arkansas LEADS/TESS Support Consultant, Arkansas School Improvement Specialist, Arkansas Quest Leadership Mentor for Administrators, Danielson Group Consultant.

Bobbie Grice, MEd; OH. Resident Educator Coordinator.

Shirley Hall, MEd; NJ. President, GreenLight for Learning, LLC; Former School and District Administrator, Danielson Group Member.

Donna Hanby, PhD; OH. Educational Consultant (Assessment & Accreditation): Educator Preparation Programs.

Kathleen Hanson, MEd; ID. Hanson Educational Consulting, Danielson Group Consultant.

MaryLou McGirr, MEd; SD. Learning Specialist, Technology & Innovation in Education; Trainer for Cognitive Coaching; Danielson Group Consultant.

Joanie Peterson, MEd; OR. Human Resources/ Professional Development Administrator; Danielson Group Consultant.

Sue Presler, MEd; NE. Training Associate, Thinking Collaborative. Trainer for Cognitive Coaching, Adaptive Schools, and Habits of Mind, Danielson Group Member.

Carol Rauch, EdD; OH. University of Cincinnati supervisor for student teachers and Associate Director of Professional Development; Danielson Group Consultant.

Cynthia M. Tocci, PhD; VA. Educational Observations, LLC, Danielson Group Director of Instructional Design.

Appendix B:
List of Study Guide Sets

Set No.	Subject	Grade
1	ELA	8
	Math	3
	Social Studies	11
2	Tech	9
	ELA	8
	Math	4
3	Math	9-10
	ELA	2
	Social Studies	7
4	ELA	12
	Math	2
	Social Studies	9
5	Science	4
	Math	11
	ELA	7
6	Math	10
	ELA	5
	Math	K
7	Math	6
	ELA	9
	Math	1
8	ELA	K
	ELA	4
	Math	9

THE
DANIELSON
GROUP

Vision

Each educator and student experiences a safe and inclusive learning environment that promotes joyful inquiry, efficacy, intellectual rigor, and reflection grounded in the Framework for Teaching.

Mission

To advance the principles of the Framework for Teaching by partnering with educators and policy leaders at all levels to strengthen professional practices and promote education policies that elevate teacher development and leadership in service of student learning.

For information about our services, or to download a free copy of the FFT Clusters document, visit our website: www.danielsongroup.org